MW01625279

SECURING THE NATION

Issues in American National Security Since 9/11

Narcotics and Terrorism

Links, Logic, and Looking Forward

SECURING THE NATION

ISSUES IN AMERICAN NATIONAL SECURITY SINCE 9/11

Intelligence: The Human Factor

Maritime and Port Security

Narcotics and Terrorism

SECURING THE NATION

ISSUES IN AMERICAN NATIONAL SECURITY SINCE 9/11

NARCOTICS AND TERRORISM

LINKS, LOGIC, AND LOOKING FORWARD

Robert B. Charles

Series Consulting Editor
Larry C. Johnson
CEO, BERG Associates, LLC
Washington, D.C.

Forewords by
Congressman J. Dennis Hastert
Speaker, U.S. House of Representatives

Former First Lady Nancy Reagan

Edwin Meese
Former Attorney General of the United States

Philadelphia

Dedicated to the Future—
May those we love live in a safer world.

CHELSEA HOUSE PUBLISHERS
VP, New Product Development Sally Cheney
Director of Production Kim Shinners
Creative Manager Takeshi Takahashi
Manufacturing Manager Diann Grasse

Staff for NARCOTICS AND TERRORISM
Editor Patrick M.N. Stone
Production Editor Megan Emery
Photo Editor Sarah Bloom
Series and Cover Designer Keith Trego
Layout 21st Century Publishing and Communications, Inc.

A Haights Cross Communications Company

www.chelseahouse.com

First Printing

1 3 5 7 9 8 6 4 2

Library of Congress Cataloging-in-Publication Data

Charles, Robert B.
Narcotics and terrorism / by Robert B. Charles.
p. cm.—(Securing the Nation)
Includes index.
Summary: Explains the changes that have occurred in national security strategies since the attacks on September 11, 2001, concerning narcotics and terrorism.
ISBN 0-7910-7701-2 (Hardcover)
1. Terrorism—Juvenile literature. 2. Narcotics and crime—Juvenile literature. 3. Drug traffic—Juvenile literature. [1. Terrorism. 2. Narcotics and crime. 3. Drug traffic.] I. Title. II. Series.
HV6431.C453 2003
363.3'2'0973—dc21

2003009501

Contents

The National Security Threat Posed by Drug Money

The link between drug money and terrorism should make every drug user pause, every American shudder, and our government redouble its efforts. Department of Justice indictments and other available information reveal that much of the money spent by Americans on illegal drugs supports those who wish to do us harm. Specifically, we know that many Middle Eastern and South American terrorist organizations profit directly from, and depend on, the sale of illegal drugs. This dependence is not slight; it enables these networks to mount serious threats to both our national security and our homeland security. It is not enough that our government appreciate this connection. Every American needs to recognize and then respond to this truth: Drug money no longer is limited to buying yachts for the kingpins, but furnishes weapons for terrorists.

In Narcotics and Terrorism: Links, Logic, and Looking Forward, Robert Charles presses the case for seeing things as they are and renewing our commitment to act against this link. He applies considerable experience—and common sense—when disposing of many dead-end notions, such as minimizing the link, legalizing dangerous narcotics, and deflecting responsibility for our individual actions.

Charles does not shy away from the reality that we live in dangerous times, and we face new, evolving national and homeland-security threats. Nor does he shy away from the truth that these are threats that we can—in fact—counteract and defeat. As a nation and as individuals, we can act to blunt the efforts of terrorists, at home and abroad, by disrupting and cutting off the money that keeps them armed and hidden. In that we do not have the option of ignoring the threat, we must not allow ourselves to ignore the solution. Only by slowing, and eventually stopping, the flow of drug money to terrorists can we effectively protect those we love. Additionally, we will save the many lives that are lost as a result of the violence in the drug trade. This is more than a laudable goal; it is a necessary act on our part.

In 1997, I stated in a congressional hearing that "powerful, wealthy, violent . . . drug cartels pose direct and insidious national security threats to this country. . . ." Today, the threat is more widely understood and much heightened. Many drug cartels are directly affiliated with several notorious, well-organized terrorist groups that despise America, and they, unlike some people in our country, are willing to act. They know what some try to ignore: that the nexus between drugs and terror is very real, very strong, and very deadly. We can overcome this, but doing so will require our utmost vigilance, energy, and commitment.

This book is a highly informative guide for anyone with an interest in the future of our nation's security, the drug war, or the health of our society. A good read, on good facts, about tough issues, with real insight—I commend it highly.

Congressman J. Dennis Hastert
Speaker, U.S. House of Representatives
June 2003

Why the Drug War and Education Remain So Important

First Lady Nancy Reagan has been a longtime advocate for drug prevention and a clear understanding of the importance of education and the drug war. She and President Ronald Reagan were leaders on this issue during their time in the White House (1981–1989). In lieu of a formal foreword for this book, Mrs. Reagan has officially authorized that portions of her unprecedented 1995 congressional testimony be used to highlight the importance of better understanding our nation's stakes in the drug war. As she said in 1995 and still believes today:

> I decided to speak . . . only after much soul searching . . . because my heart pulls me . . . and because my husband and everything he stands for calls me. . . . I'm worried that this nation is forgetting how endangered our children are by drugs. I'm worried that for the first time in many years, tolerance for drugs and the mistaken perception that "everyone is doing it" is creeping back into our national mentality. And I am worried that the psychological momentum we had against drug use is being lost.
>
> And yet it is more than worry. This weakening vigilance against the drug threat has obviously been a disappointment to me, but more importantly it can have a tragic effect on this country for many years to come.

So, yes—I'm worried about the future of our young people. I'm disappointed, and yes, I'm saddened. How could we have forgotten so quickly? Why is it we no longer hear the drumbeat of condemnation against drugs coming from our leaders and our culture? Is it any wonder drug use has started climbing again and dramatically so?

With my own eyes, I've seen the human destruction drugs can cause. During my eight years as First Lady, I traveled hundreds of thousands of miles around this country and the world meeting with young people, listening to the heartbreaking stories of what drugs did to their lives. That suffering is something I can never forget.

When I spoke to gatherings across the country, I often read letters from young people who were facing personal struggles with drug use. I did it for a specific reason. I wanted to educate this country about the savage toll that drugs were inflicting upon children. I wanted to make sure people couldn't ignore the tragic human consequences of drug use.

I'm afraid we must start reminding people all over again. . . . I am absolutely distraught when I think of what is happening to so many children across America. We must give them the motivation and support to say "no" to drugs. We must correct the perception that "everyone is doing it." And we must teach them the skills to recognize and resist the pressure to use drugs.

Before the drug increases of 1993 and 1994, we really had seen marked progress. A decade of effort was beginning to pay off. Attitudes were being changed. Monthly cocaine use dropped from nearly three million users in 1988 to 1.3 million users in 1990. It's the same story with other numbers: Between 1991 and 1992, overall drug use dropped from 14.5 million users to 11.4 million. . . . I don't mean to . . . say that we had won the battle against drugs. I think it's plain we have not. Even so, the battle was going forward with the help of athletes and entertainers, and many CEO's of large companies. . . . There was momentum, unity, intolerance of the exaggeration and glorification of drug use by the media—in short, there was progress. . . .

Children were beginning to understand that government leaders, actors, musicians and sports figures typically don't use drugs. And they were being taught resistance skills. Where has this social influence model and this support . . . gone? Where is the widespread consensus that was backing the children up, and giving them the motivation and skills they needed? How could we have abandoned that? . . .

If there is a clear and forceful no-use message coming from strong, outspoken leadership—it *is* potent. Half-hearted commitment does not work. This drift, this complacency, in our nation's commitment to prevention is what led me [to speak out]. . . . Let me say that many of you[,] . . . Republicans and Democrats alike, share my deep concern that we have lost the momentum. We have lost a sense of priority on this problem; we have lost all sense of national urgency and leadership. . . .

The real solution is to dry up demand, and that can only come through education and strong moral leadership. It can only come through prevention. . . . But it all requires leadership . . . in Washington [also]. Where has it gone? It seems as though this country has lost its drive to keep the drug issue—and especially drug prevention—in the national spotlight. Today, the anti-drug message just seems to be fading away. Children [and all of us, in a world where drug money helps to fund terrorism]* need to hear it, and hear it often. . . .

In closing, let me say that people often ask me what I miss most about our eight years in the White House. In retrospect, I think what I miss most is the sense of common national purpose that so many of us felt. . . . What has happened to our common national purpose on drugs? And how do we get it back?

We need to educate this generation and all future generations. . . .

Former First Lady Nancy Reagan
June 2003

* Note: Bracketed information has been added by editor.

Health, Criminal Justice, and National Security

When I was attorney general of the United States, under President Ronald Reagan, drug abuse was viewed as a vital health, criminal justice, and national security concern. The tie between the criminal element and foreign terrorists was only just coming into view, but the importance of tracing and stopping the flow of drug money back to foreign sources was paramount. Today, this mission is as important as ever—in a world in which we are coming to know more about the actual and likely ties between drug traffickers and global terrorist networks.

This book, Narcotics and Terrorism: Links, Logic, and Looking Forward, by Robert Charles, a former Reagan and Bush White House staffer, federal law clerk, and counsel to Speaker of the House J. Dennis Hastert, should be on everyone's "must read" list, if they see—or if they do not yet see, but nevertheless care about—the growing connection between drug trafficking proceeds and international terrorism.

In short, this is a direct, punchy, readable presentation of facts that are seldom brought together in one place. The breadth of terrorist movements and how they pay for the terror they spread is coupled with a clear-headed discussion of worldwide drug trafficking, reasons why drug legalization will never work, and the best prospects for a sustainable, long-term policy—as well as guidance for good individual decision-making.

Here is an extract from the larger debates about drug policy, criminal justice, national security, and personal responsibility that leaves one refreshed and renewed—aware that good decisions can and should be made by those who hold power and, ultimately, by all citizens. Moreover, the making of good decisions in this realm will produce a healthier, stronger, more secure, and less vulnerable society. The facts are compelling. The analysis by Robert Charles is both thorough and incisive. His message seems almost self-evident, yet inspires the reader anew: The efforts against drug trafficking and terrorism are both well worth it; indeed, Americans have a duty to fight these twin evils wherever they find them. These battles are also winnable, by increments, through education, priority setting, and a combination of individual and national conviction. In these pages you will find a persuasive analysis, together with a strong set of current facts, for all who care about the future of our country.

I offer one other thought. The issues that we confront as a nation today are a variation of issues that we faced more than a decade ago. We make progress not without sacrifice and loss, but with endurance and conviction. In 1992, I wrote: "Although the production, trafficking, and use of illegal drugs are still a serious problem in our nation and throughout the world, significant change occurred pursuant to Reagan's firm stand against drugs." In fact, statistics indicate that use of any illicit drug by high-school seniors dropped from 54 percent in 1979, the year before President Reagan took office, to 29 percent in 1991, two years after he left office. This constitutes a drop of over 45 percent.

Additionally, in 1991, 90 percent of high-school seniors disapproved of even trying LSD, barbiturates, cocaine, or heroin, and nearly 70 percent disapproved of trying marijuana. These were healthy, smart attitudes and they differed markedly from the sad experiences of those in the 1960s and 1970s. Though the nation faces new challenges in 2003, the chances for success are as strong as ever. Although highly pure heroin, cocaine, and marijuana, as well as Ecstasy and rave drugs, threaten our youth, culture, and security, common sense and serious efforts to turn around drug use can be as successful now as they have been in the past.

Notably, when I wrote in 1992, I merged this discussion of drug trafficking with another issue of importance to the nation, even at that time. I noted that, "perhaps the most frightening form of crime in the modern era is terrorism. . . ." To this observation, I offered context. For a variety of reasons, "the Reagan government initiated a major effort to combat both international and domestic terrorism." We learned that vigilance pays off. In 1992, that early antiterrorism effort allowed me to later reflect: "As with street crime and drugs, the data showed the impact of our efforts against terrorism. . . . The number of terrorist incidents in the U.S. dropped from 112 in 1979 to only seven in 1985 and eight in 1986. . . . In 1985 alone, the FBI detected and prevented twenty-three separate terrorist missions within the borders of the United States—and did so without violating anybody's 'civil liberties.'"

In short, this volume reinforces what we know has historically worked. Prevention and education, law enforcement support, treatment and rehabilitation, and a focus on international cooperation—made more critical by tightening bonds between the drug traffickers and terrorists—will allow this nation again to bring down these threats to our long-term security, and to the freedom of our people.

Edwin Meese
Former Attorney General of the United States
June 2003

Introduction

The horrific attacks of September 11 changed forever our generation's sense of security. Although terrorism is not a new phenomenon, most Americans thought of terrorism as something that showed up in Hollywood movies. International terrorists rarely carried out attacks inside the United States. We were complacent.

When the first plane hit the northern tower of the World Trade Center, our complacency vanished. We now understand in some measure what our grandparents and great-grandparents felt when Pearl Harbor was attacked. We have felt firsthand the shock, bewilderment, confusion, and fear that they certainly felt upon hearing that the U.S. Navy's fleet at Pearl Harbor was bombed on Sunday morning, December 7, 1941.

Our own "date which will live in infamy," however, was more traumatic—not because more people died, but because we all witnessed the terrible events. Unlike our grandparents, most of whom learned of Pearl Harbor through secondhand sources—the radio or newspapers—we saw it happen live and, initially, unfiltered. We shared part of the experience of the people who were actually at or near the World Trade Center or the Pentagon on that fateful morning. Everyone who was near a television witnessed the burning buildings, the collapsing towers, and the fleeing crowds. We did not have to *imagine* fear, for we *saw* it.

The shock of the event was accompanied in short order by an overwhelming sense of vulnerability and the start of a search for how this could happen. Fear remained a dominant emotion. Images of troops in the streets in Washington, D.C., and New York City and combat air patrols by jet fighters reinforced the impression that we were under siege. Rather than venture out of the house, many stayed home. Airports and train stations were vacant. Business travel and tourism dropped precipitously.

In the succeeding months we have become acquainted with color-coded threat systems and witnessed the creation of new government institutions, such as the Transportation Security Agency and the Department of Homeland Security.

September 11 transformed America and its citizens. As the shock subsided and we coped with our fears, our attention shifted to explaining how the attack had been accomplished, punishing those responsible, and fixing the vulnerabilities that had enabled the attack to succeed. Americans—citizens and pundits alike—began asking questions: What would it take to make the United States truly secure? Is security a realistic objective, or are we chasing an illusion? What is the nature of the threat or threats that we are confronting? To stop religious extremists, are we willing to empower the federal government to spy on churches, mosques, or synagogues? How can we achieve effective national security and still remain a free people?

The books in SECURING THE NATION may not provide complete answers to these questions; some questions probably cannot be answered at all. But these books *will* equip the reader with knowledge about the security changes that are currently under way in the United States and will enable the reader to think and speak intelligently about issues of national security.

We are living in a historical moment, a period of time during which an event or series of events sets in motion forces that will shape the future, the world of the next generation. The bombing of Pearl Harbor, the Holocaust, the destruction of Hiroshima and Nagasaki by atomic bombs, the assassination of President John F. Kennedy in November of 1963—all were historical moments. The terrorist attack of September 11 and the invasion of Iraq are historical moments, too. We are living in the midst of changes that years from now will be viewed by our children or grandchildren as watershed events.

COULD 9/11 HAVE BEEN PREVENTED?

Were the 9/11 hijackings an unexpected "bolt from the blue"? No, not really. Even though most Americans were unfamiliar with Osama bin Laden, Al Qaeda, and the radical Islamic terrorist training camps in Afghanistan, the intelligence community and the law enforcement community were well aware of these threats. Have you ever tried to put together a jigsaw puzzle? If you have the pieces of the puzzle, you can assemble the picture with concerted effort. If pieces are missing, the puzzle will be impossible to complete. In the aftermath of 9/11 we discovered that we'd had the clues all along, that information on the threat posed by bin Laden and his followers had been collected—but that those clues had been scattered among different government agencies and organizations. The agencies had not shared their puzzle pieces with one another.

A more specific example of this "failure to communicate" can be found in the Bojinka plot of 1995. In January of that year, Filipino police and firefighters accidentally stumbled upon a group of terrorists trying to make explosives in their apartment in downtown Manila. The subsequent investigation revealed that this group included one Abdul Basit, the man who had planned and carried out the first bombing of the World Trade Center in February of 1993. Basit managed to elude the Filipino police, but one of his partners, Hakim Murad, was arrested. When Murad was interrogated, he revealed that he, Basit, and three others had planned to plant bombs on commercial jets and blow them up in mid-flight. The conspirators had intended to execute their plot, which they had code-named "Bojinka," toward the end of that same January.

This information was passed to the Federal Bureau of Investigation (FBI), which was assisting the investigation. The FBI considered as its mission to gather evidence that could ultimately be presented before a judge and jury in order to convict the terrorists—not to share this information with other agencies. Neither did the FBI feel that it had a responsibility to warn American air carriers about the possible attack. Many FBI agents involved with the case believed that sharing this information would compromise the FBI's case and prevent the prosecution of the terrorist in custody.

Meanwhile, Central Intelligence Agency (CIA) operatives in Manila discovered the Bojinka plot and published an intelligence report. The report was then disseminated throughout Washington agencies and departments, including the Department of State, the Department of Defense, and the Federal Aviation Administration (FAA). This CIA report sparked a dispute among the agencies over whether to inform the American air carriers about the threat; at a meeting convened in late January, representatives from the various departments argued heatedly over what to do with this information. The FBI feared that releasing the information to the airlines would compromise its ability to prosecute the terrorists who had hatched the plot and was therefore strongly against sharing. For the State Department and the FAA, the goal was to use intelligence to warn the airliners about a threat and to take steps to prevent an attack. Thus, the FBI was pitted against the State Department, the FAA, and the CIA; ultimately, the decision was made to warn the airlines. No attack is known to have occurred.

This story of the discovery of the Bojinka plot and the

uphill battle to share the information obtained from the investigation illustrates the processes and bureaucratic cultures that allowed 9/11 to happen. I am not assigning blame or fault to any particular organization. Rather, I want to emphasize that although we have one government, it is made up of a variety of departments and agencies, each of which has a unique way of looking at the world. It is possible for each department to work to the best of its ability to do its job properly but, in the end, only help to create a disaster. The law enforcement mentality sees its task as one of acquiring and preserving evidence with the ultimate goal of convicting a suspect in a court of law. The work of a criminal investigation is compartmented—in other words, only those directly involved with the case will have access to the evidence collected. Given that an organization like the FBI conducts thousands of criminal investigations every year, it becomes easy to appreciate that no one person or group of persons can fully understand the various cases being pursued.

In the aftermath of 9/11, we learned more disturbing facts. An FBI office in Minnesota had tried unsuccessfully in August of 2001 to obtain a subpoena to examine a computer used by Zaccarias Moussai, who was taking flying lessons but had shown no interest in learning to perform takeoffs or landings. Earlier in 2001, the FBI office in Arizona had submitted a request to investigate foreign Muslims who were taking flying lessons and acting suspiciously. This request also had been rejected. Then we learned that the FBI's debriefing of Hakim Murad in January 1995 had revealed that the terrorists had planned to hijack commercial airliners in the United States and fly them into CIA headquarters—and we came to the sickening realization that we'd had key clues in our hands and had not understood them or acted on them. Many law enforcement agents had recognized the potential threat, but their efforts to attract attention to the information had been blocked by bureaucratic procedures and also by individuals who had not appreciated the magnitude of the threat.

The intelligence community failed to process the clues and act in time to prevent the attack; here again, as with the example of the FBI, we have learned that there was plenty of information available. In January of 2001, for example, CIA officers in Malaysia monitored a meeting that included individuals who later hijacked the planes on 9/11. The CIA claims its agents passed this information to the FBI, but it appears that the intelligence was sent through an informal e-mail. In order to be taken seriously, information sent between agencies must be sent in the proper format. In this case, the informal nature of the communication resulted in the information's "falling between the cracks."

From the perspective of the intelligence community, it is important to protect information in order to hide the identity of the sources. Unlike the FBI, which is focused on collecting evidence to build a specific case, the intelligence community generates volumes of more general information. Genuine intelligence analysts are paid to sift through the information flood and to extract important data, much like a gold prospector who crouches over a stream for hours at a time, filtering out mud and water to find the occasional nugget of gold. But the task is greater than just *collecting* the information; the pieces of intelligence must also be assembled, analyzed, interpreted, and molded into a coherent story.

The ability of CIA and FBI analysts to predict or even fully analyze terrorist threats has been restricted, however, by limitations on the kinds of intelligence these agencies can collect and analyze. In the late 1960s and early 1970s, President Richard Nixon ordered the FBI and the CIA to gather information about his political enemies, and these abuses led to reforms that prevented the FBI from collecting intelligence on American citizens without evidence of a possible crime. The reforms also limited the CIA's ability to operate domestically; consequently, the powers of the CIA and FBI to conduct domestic intelligence activities were scaled back dramatically. Since then, the CIA has focused its attention and resources on threats outside the United States, and the FBI has emphasized building specific cases for prosecution. In the years before 9/11, no agency or department of the United States government had the power to collect and analyze intelligence about terrorist activities *within* the United States that were being directed by *foreign-based* entities.

The problem of information sharing between the FBI and the CIA becomes even more profound once we understand that the law enforcement community and the intelligence community both comprise multiple agencies. The law enforcement community, for example, includes the U.S. Customs Service, the Drug Enforcement Administration (DEA), the Internal Revenue Service (IRS), the Secret Service, the U.S. Marshals, the Bureau of Alcohol, Tobacco, Firearms, and Explosives (ATF), and the U.S. Park Police. Each agency has the power to conduct federal criminal investigations, and no central system exists to organize all the information the agencies collect. In fact, there have been numerous instances in which multiple agencies pursued the same target. In 1991, for instance, DEA agents arrested Dandeny Muñoz ("La Quika") Mosquera for drug trafficking and money laundering. Mosquera, who had planned the bombing of an Avianca commercial airplane in Colombia in November of 1989, also was the target of an terrorist investigation led by the FBI. Rather than cooperate in the investigation, the two federal agencies pursued the target independently, with DEA winning the race.

The intelligence community, though not as large, is equally diverse. In addition to the CIA, there is the Defense Intelligence Agency (DIA), the National Security Agency (NSA), the National Reconnaissance Office (NRO), various intelligence outfits in the

U.S. military's regional commands, the Department of Energy (DOE), and the FAA. The CIA, DIA, NSA, and NRO specialize in intelligence collection, which means they use either human spies or technology to intercept signals. Once this information is obtained, it is turned into a finished product, much like a newspaper article, and distributed to policymakers and intelligence analysts in other organizations. In highly sensitive cases, however, there is some information that is not shared with other organizations.

The law enforcement and intelligence communities both knew that Osama bin Laden and his followers were responsible for previous attacks and were planning future attacks. Unfortunately, the hunt for bin Laden and the effort to prevent future attacks were neither coordinated nor focused: Each organization pursued the target using its own resources and according to its own goals. In the mid-1990s, for instance, the government of the Republic of the Sudan offered to hand bin Laden over to American authorities. The offer was handled primarily by the Department of Justice and the Department of State, rather than through a "full-court" effort by the entire government. According to one of those involved in brokering the potential deal, it fell apart over the fact that no one at the Justice Department believed a solid, prosecutable case could be brought against bin Laden based on the evidence available at that time.

After 9/11, we learned that there were numerous serious indicators of an impending attack but that the information had been scattered among too many agencies to form a meaningful picture. Parts of the Al Qaeda network had even been penetrated by the U.S. government, but we had failed to pay attention to available intelligence and to act on it in a decisive, coordinated way.

Thus there were *two* important failures that paved the way for 9/11—not only the failure to share information between the intelligence community and the law enforcement community, but also a failure of analysis. We had the key pieces of the puzzle, but we failed to put them together. Because of these twin failures, the Twin Towers collapsed, the Pentagon was partially burned, and a plane fell in a Pennsylvania field after valiant passengers struggled to wrest control of the aircraft from its hijackers.

PUNISHING THOSE RESPONSIBLE

The terrorist attack of September 11 awakened the slumbering United States from years of apathy. We discovered in early 1995 that Osama bin Laden was linked to the terrorists who had bombed the World Trade Center in 1993. With attacks by Islamic militants against the U.S. military's housing complex in Dharan, Saudi Arabia, and the August 1998 bombings of the American embassies in Kenya and Tanzania, it became clear that we were at war with bin Laden. Bin Laden and his followers, who were based in Afghanistan, were training warriors for *jihad*—Islamic holy war against Western infidels—and plotting new offensives. President Bill Clinton launched cruise missile strikes against Al Qaeda training facilities in August of 1998, but the missile strikes inflicted little damage on the terrorists. When they attacked the U.S.S. *Cole* off the coast of Yemen in October of 2000, the United States did nothing. The terrorists considered the United States a weak nation, one incapable of defending itself.

It was not until nineteen Islamic militants simultaneously attacked the nation on September 11 that the United States found the motivation to mount a significant response. President Bush and his national security team immediately began to plan the nation's strategy. The immediate problem was the terrorist training camps in Afghanistan, so within days U.S. intelligence and special-operations personnel were on the ground in that country. They forged ties with opponents of the

Taliban, the main regime that was harboring bin Laden and his Al Qaeda followers. Two months after the September 11 attack, U.S. military operations were under way in Afghanistan, successfully routing both the Taliban and Al Qaeda.

The success of the war in Afghanistan proved to be the first and least difficult phase in the "war on terror." Not only were the training camps destroyed, but American forces captured Islamic radicals, documents, and computers that in turn provided law enforcement and intelligence with an information bonanza. Unlike previous failed efforts, the FBI and CIA now joined forces to work together in genuine partnership. An interagency team established operations centers throughout the upper floors of the J. Edgar Hoover Building, the FBI's headquarters, which sits six blocks east of the White House. In addition to FBI agents, the task forces were staffed by representatives from U.S. Customs, the Department of the Treasury, the ATF, the IRS, the Secret Service, the U.S. Marshals, the NSA, the CIA, the DOE, and the NRO. It was a veritable "alphabet soup" of government agencies and an important attempt at cooperation.

With the destruction of Al Qaeda training camps in Afghanistan, the number of viable military targets for counterterrorist operations decreased dramatically. As a result, the focus shifted to intelligence and law enforcement operations, both domestic and international. The investigation of Al Qaeda revealed a multilayered organization with support cells and adherents in numerous countries. Working with foreign police and intelligence operatives, U.S. agents set to work in hundreds of regions around the world. Financial investigations revealed covert support to terrorist operations from Islamic charities based in the United States. Other terrorists were caught engaging in more mundane criminal activities, such as cigarette smuggling.

The capture of key members of Al Qaeda provided further

leads in the search for additional collaborators. A few of those apprehended were subjected to conventional arrest, and many more are being held in military detention centers. Since 9/11, the United States has entered new legal territory in several domains, among which is prisoners' rights. The terrorists in custody are treated humanely according to the standards of the Geneva Convention, but they are denied the legal rights granted to prisoners of war. By removing the terrorists from society, the United States has disrupted their ability to plan new attacks, recruit new followers, and kill more innocent civilians; it is no coincidence that in 2002 international terrorist attacks fell to their lowest level in 34 years.

FIXING THE VULNERABILITIES

The lack of information sharing between and among government agencies and the failure to act on information in our possession were not the only shortcomings that the 9/11 attack revealed. In the aftermath, we finally acknowledged that many of our security systems were inadequate and underfunded. For example, the hijackings were *not* a consequence of inadequate work by security screeners; in fact, the security companies that guarded the screening checkpoints at Logan and Dulles Airports did their job properly and permitted on the aircraft only items that were acceptable by existing security standards. Before September 12, 2001, modeling knives were allowed aboard commercial airliners.

The Al Qaeda terrorists did not defeat the aviation security systems that were in place on September 11, so much as exploit the gaps in those systems. Although not heavily armed, the terrorists ensured that at least four members of their group were aboard each plane. They selected domestic flights with the full understanding that international flights would be more likely to be guarded by air marshals. They also knew that they did not *have* to be heavily armed. They could hijack a plane simply by announcing an intention to do so and threatening the pilots, flight attendants, and passengers—brandishing even something as innocuous as a fountain pen or a cylindrical tube.

The aviation security system of the time was based on the belief that even if someone hijacked a plane by threatening to detonate a bomb, the crew, especially the pilots, would stay in control of the plane because hijackers were not pilots. September 11 exposed this assumption as false. Not only had some of the hijackers undergone training as pilots, but they also were suicidal—preserving their own lives was *not* among their goals.

The flight crews on 9/11 acted in accordance with their training. They did their jobs bravely. Pilots and flight attendants had been taught to handle hijackers in much the way that a bank teller is taught to deal with a bank robber—to cooperate, to surrender what the aggressor wants, and to stall as much as possible in the hope that reinforcements will arrive. On 9/11, we learned the hard way that this training was not a valid way of handling a modern hijacking—and that fuel-filled planes could very easily be transformed into human-controlled cruise missiles.

Since the 9/11 hijackings, the federal government has been taking concrete steps to prevent such a thing from ever happening again. Aboard commercial airliners, there was a fundamental shift in the ways in which flight crews were taught to respond to a hijacking. Rather than cooperating and granting hijackers access to the cockpit, pilots now remain behind a locked door. The doors have been hardened to withstand, albeit temporarily, attempts to open them, even those attempts that use bullets or hand grenades. A hardened door buys the pilots time; with luck, the extra time will enable them to take the aircraft down to an altitude that will minimize the risk of a catastrophic decompression if the skin of the aircraft is breached. In addition, pilots now are authorized to carry a pistol and have the last-resort option of being able to open a lockbox, remove a handgun, and defend the plane from being taken over if a hijacker succeeds in bypassing the door.

Significant changes in aviation security have also occurred on the ground. The responsibility for security screening has been taken away from private contractors and put into the hands of the U.S. government's new Transportation Security Agency. Money has been appropriated to purchase and deploy explosive-detection systems to check luggage for bombs. Passengers traveling by air today have a much greater guarantee that the trip will be safe and more secure.

Improving aviation security was relatively easy because a "roadmap" for the process already existed. Previous reports issued under both Republican and Democratic administrations—the *Report of the President's Commission on Aviation Security and Terrorism* (1990) and the *White House Commission Report on Aviation Safety and Security* (1997) had identified the problems and recommended solutions.

But securing the nation is not a simple proposition, and there is no easy "roadmap." America's sense of vulnerability was magnified by 9/11 and by the wave of anthrax attacks that followed it—which remain unexplained even now. Regardless of the cause, the spate of infections highlighted the fact that the existing system for handling and delivering postal mail did not include safeguards or systems for detecting and preventing the movement of hazardous materials. The federal government responded rapidly by installing equipment to detect and disinfect suspicious mail. Also, new measures were adopted for improving communications with local public-health departments and the Centers for Disease Control and Prevention (CDC), the main federal institution charged with protecting the public from disease.

Out of this chaos, the Bush administration conceived of a

broader vision of national security. In a move that recalls the National Security Act of 1948, which led to the creation of the Department of Defense and the Central Intelligence Agency, the Bush administration proposed establishing what it called the Department of Homeland Security. This federal department consists of agencies drawn from the Department of the Treasury (e.g., the Secret Service, the U.S. Customs Service), the Department of Justice (e.g., the Immigration and Naturalization Service), the Department of Transportation (e.g., the Coast Guard, the Federal Aviation Administration), and the Department of Energy. In theory, the new department will provide any administration with the ability to establish a clear security budget for protecting the nation. This reorganization is intended to reduce the overlap in agency activities and enable the federal government to focus scarce resources on specific problems.

With the arrival of the Department of Homeland Security comes a central mechanism for dealing with a variety of security tasks that previously were dealt with in a haphazard, uncoordinated way. The responsibility for ensuring that there are plans and standards for protecting nuclear power plants, seaports, public transportation (including buses, subways, and commuter trains), public water systems, and electrical grids is now fairly straightforward. This does not mean that the task is simple, though. The Department of Homeland Security represents a collection of agencies and personnel, and the difficulty of managing it will rival the challenge of managing the Department of Defense.

Less dramatic but equally important reforms are under way at the CIA and the FBI, the FBI's transformation being the greater of the two. Before 9/11, for example, documents and records that the FBI obtained in the course of a criminal investigation would lie dormant in boxes; they were never converted to electronic files that could be searched using current data mining technology. Under the leadership of Robert Mueller, the FBI has established a unit on the top floor of its headquarters, the J. Edgar Hoover Building, that is dedicated to scanning the millions of documents that the agency collects. The database resulting from this scanning effort is large already and growing. It offers to investigators a previously unavailable resource for finding links between terrorists and mundane criminals. In addition, the FBI has set up several different task force operation centers that are staffed around the clock and include representatives from other agencies.

President Bush also directed the FBI and the CIA to create a joint threat-monitoring and threat-assessment center. Both agencies initially resisted this plan, but both relented under persistent pressure from the president and his advisors. Providing one place where threat information from domestic and international sources can be evaluated cooperatively and analyzed for links will bridge the gap that enabled critical warning intelligence to go unnoticed in the weeks and months prior to 9/11.

CONCLUSION

The books in SECURING THE NATION provide a comprehensive introduction to the changes that have taken place in American national security since the terrorist attack of September 11. The current issues in national security are discussed by experts who have worked extensively to resolve those issues. Certainly, there is nothing wrong with an academic viewpoint—but theoreticians who have no grounding in practice often have difficulty in finding the roots of the issues they study. The authors in this series, in contrast, are thoughtful practitioners. They have served their country as military officers and government officials. They have grappled with the problems of developing and implementing new policies amid intense bureaucratic battles. Some have been sent on top-secret missions by presidents—many of which remain highly classified.

As you read and debate the information in these books, I encourage you to think critically. The publication of a piece of information does not make that information true. Be quick to ask why, and insist on hard, empirical evidence to corroborate or refute a statement claimed as fact. Hopefully, you will discover that national security is not based on deploying the most technologically sophisticated metal detector or hiring thousands of new specialists—but on freedom and the rule of law. The freedoms we enjoy belong to citizens who know their rights and understand how their government works.

The surprise attack on Pearl Harbor in 1941 produced a reaction of fear, a fear that ultimately was invoked to justify confiscating the property of Japanese Americans and jailing them in concentration camps. Even though the United States was at war with Germany and Italy as well as Japan, the federal government targeted only citizens of Japanese heritage, possibly because they were the most "different." The September 11 hijackers were Islamic radicals from Saudi Arabia and Egypt, so 9/11 created a similar opportunity to target Arab Americans. The Bush administration made a conscious effort after 9/11 to ensure that Arab Americans were not defined as a threat, so the nation was not subjected to another episode of internment or widespread persecution. But the analogy illustrates the need for citizens to understand issues of national security: Lapses in security can and *have* been used to justify restricting the civil liberties of American citizens. Consider the ideas in these books, use them to build your understanding of the federal government's operations, and make the choice to play a constructive role in securing the nation.

Larry C. Johnson
CEO, BERG Associates, LLC
Washington, D.C.

1

Narcotics and Terrorism: Fin and Jaws

Understanding the relationship between terrorism and narcotics is a bit like watching the angular fin of a shark surface—suddenly and silently on a calm day. In the North Atlantic's chilly waters, I have seen it happen, stood above the ripples. You know at once the serious connection between this enabling fin and those jagged, unseen jaws, but you do not see the whole picture. If you did, it would be too late. If you waited for further proof, you would no longer need it or benefit from the certainty you gained. When the fin disappears, you get that quiet, false sense of relief. You jerk yourself back—the shark is still there. The wake left by its fin dissipates, returning the world to a sense of normal. Like time's soothing balm in the aftermath of a terrorist attack, we convince ourselves that the worst is past. But the fin and jaws are still there, still on the hunt, still working together for the next approach and possible attack.

Like the tie between terrorism and narcotics, we ignore the fin—and jaws—at our peril. Only by continuous investigation, quick eyes, smart decisions under constant pressure, and the unwavering commitment *not* to forget can we be sure that—when the shark circles in again—we will be ready. We will know the shark for what it is, and we will be prepared. What is more, by knowing the connection, it will not make us its prey.

Unfortunately, since the tragic events of September 11, 2001, the link between drugs and terrorism has become even more important. At the same time, it has been variously ignored, oversimplified, overstated, and under-analyzed.

This short book offers a snapshot of the actual relationship between narcotics and terrorism, nuts and bolts, groups, places, methods of operation, indictments, and implications surrounding that relationship. No classified or "law enforcement–sensitive" information is used in this account, but we cover a substantial body of open-source (that is, unclassified) information here.

This book will offer strong evidence for the following propositions:

- Drug trafficking and terrorism are bound to one another through recruiting pools, financing, geography, international crime (for example, arms traffickers), impact on our day-to-day security, and, at times, even motivation;
- Drug traffickers and terrorists share a common indifference to the sanctity of human life, radiating circles of death and suffering to innocent persons caught in their webs;
- Worldwide trends in drug trafficking and terrorism suggest a convergence of drug traffickers and recognized terrorist groups;
- Traditional markets for illegal drugs in the United States and Europe are being expanded to fill a funding void created by lost "state sponsors";
- Terrorists and drug traffickers are, by design and coincidence, adding significant costs to major sectors of the world economy, from health care to law enforcement, including key sectors of the U.S. economy;
- Policy solutions can be found, including greater education and vigilance on both drug use and terrorism,

reinforcement of U.S. borders, support for state and local law enforcement, more international cooperation, and a well-publicized recognition of the links between narcotics and terrorism;

- Policy distractions, such as indulging arguments for "peace at all costs," "justifiable terrorism," or legalizing addictive substances, will leave us wishing we had exercised better judgment. Such alluring eddies place at risk the long-term safety, security, and health of our society, at best serving only as examples of policy failure. In the language of metaphor, to see the fin and ignore the jaws would be a profound mistake;

- The prevalence of narcotics and terrorism in our global society has ebbed and flowed in proportion to our public commitment to confront these two menaces. Tackling the purveyors of such palpable evil is an unending and often unsavory mission; to think otherwise would be short-sighted and unrealistic. On the other hand, success—defined as a more secure, safer, and healthier society—is worth the effort. No one likes to find a shark in the water, but when one does, it is best to reach for the gaff;

- In short, seeing a clear link between terrorism and narcotics—recognizing that the fin and jaws come together, work together, endanger together—should give us warning. Seeing the link clearly should stiffen our resolve to confront *both* threats on multiple fronts. These threats cannot be separated; nevertheless, they *can* be turned back as surely as we have beaten similar threats to human security, safety, and health. To diminish or ignore obvious

> linkages is to underestimate their combined impact. Separately and together, they affect our culture and on our day-to-day lives. It is easy to think of the two—narcotics and terrorism—as unrelated; sadly, they are not. Without a dorsal fin, the shark's jaws cannot strike. With a dorsal fin, the shark is a formidable predator.

In the pages ahead, you will find four principal discussions. The first concerns definitions: What is terrorism? What are the leading terrorist organizations? How does illegal drug consumption in America and Europe weave its way into these organizations? What types of illegal drugs are known to finance terrorism? What do we know about these drugs and the networks that support their distribution?

Second, what are the geographic, political, and financial links between drug trafficking groups and terrorist groups? Do their memberships overlap, and if so, how much and in what way? Are they tied to international criminal organizations that traffic in arms, children, and contraband? How close are these relationships? Do they reinforce one another?

Third, what trends can we read in the passage of time? Are terrorist and drug trafficking organizations converging, and if so how? What implications should that have for U.S. law enforcement and national security? How about for U.S. diplomacy and the way we work with other nations? Do these trends tell us anything about how we should live our own lives?

Fourth, are there sound policy solutions—real answers—to these problems? Are there distractions that we are better off avoiding? What are the costs of different policy options, and the costs of delaying, deferring, or ignoring decisions when tackling the link between these two menaces? In formal economic terms and by reference to common sense, is drug legalization an answer, illusion, or dangerous error with long-term consequences?

2

Who Are Terrorists?

Finding definitions on which *all* readers will agree is probably not possible, but let's start with some basics. Illegal narcotics, or illegal drugs, are defined by federal law (typically found in the U.S. Criminal Code). Accordingly, there is no mystery here. Illegal narcotics include, for example, heroin, crack cocaine, cocaine hydrochloride, methamphetamine, methylenedioxymethamphetamine (MDMA or Ecstasy), phencyclidine (PCP), gamma-hydroxy butyrate (GHB or "the date-rape drug"), lysergic acid diethylamide (LSD), tetrahydrocannibinol (the active compound in marijuana), and various other opiates, cannabinoids, and synthetic drugs, including prescription medications for which there is no medically justified possession.

By contrast, the acts and organizations that qualify as "terrorism" can be more difficult to isolate, accurately define, and catalog. In general, federal law defines terrorism as premeditated, politically motivated violence against noncombatant (civilian) targets by subnational groups or clandestine agents.[1] That said, agreement is not always clear. Generally, certain tenets survive both public discussion and official government review. To paraphrase one of Supreme Court Justice Potter Stewart's ideas on obscenity, most people know it when they see it.[2] In that way, shark jaws and terrorism are alike: Once you see them, there is no mistaking what you have seen.

WHAT IS TERRORISM?

Somehow, after the horror of passenger airliners crashing into the Twin Towers and the Pentagon, and a terrorist-controlled airliner being brought down in a field in rural Pennsylvania, terrorism is no longer theoretical. It is real—vivid and palpable—and will stay that way for as long as any of us lives.

No less real are images of Middle Eastern terrorists detonating suicide bombs in Israel, Africa, Iraq, Bali, Saudi Arabia, and Yemen, on buses, in cafés, at American embassies, at the side of the U.S.S. *Cole,* and at various border checkpoints. The resulting human carnage—innocent lives suddenly and violently lost in acts of utter barbarism—is obviously outside the political process and civil order. Such events cannot fail to spur serious reflection, anger, sadness, and policy review.

We ask ourselves how this could happen. We redefine our own safety by the new vulnerability these acts portend. They are too close for comfort; there is no looking away. Terrorism *is* part of our world. The choices we make and the degree of vigilance we exercise will affect us all.

A few common points can be identified among terrorist acts. Typically, acts of terrorism are:

- conducted with the intent to cause death or suffering to innocent persons (with full knowledge or an expectation that the acts will do so);
- motivated by a mixture of hatred, anger, resentment, greed, or political, ideological, or religious extremism perceived to justify violence toward others;
- intended to create terror or fear in those who live to see the violent, inhumane acts completed;
- accompanied by some degree of training and preparation; that is, conducted with planning and "malice aforethought";

- coordinated with others who are wholly or partly informed about the intent of the perpetrator; and
- financed in whole or part by states, organizations, or individuals who know that the funds provided will assist in underwriting terrorist acts.

This traditional, largely "operational," definition of terrorism is one of many ways to describe the illegal, anticivilized acts that fall under the general heading of "terrorism."

Looking beyond the binding of this book, there are categories of acts that may in their own right *deserve* to be labeled as terrorism, but that generally are not thought of as terrorism. For example, consider the following questions:

- Outside the context of a declared war between two nations (which is subject to the protections and limitations of the Geneva Convention), could we say that any act of threatening to take an innocent life, let alone causing death—even one—is an act of terrorism? Must the act be politically, ideologically, or religiously motivated? Could there not be an "act of terror" motivated by personal greed, ruthlessness, or sheer indifference to human life?
- What about unlawful acts intended to control the life of another—through threats, coercion, torture, or the imposition of other physical harm? Do such acts not amount to "terrorism," whether carried out by a government, organization, or individual?
- What about unlawful acts intended to trigger a behavior that may result in the subject's death? Are these acts not reasonably considered "terrorism?" If they are, can we sensibly argue also that those who knowingly distribute deadly narcotics, like those who knowingly create suicide bombers out of the unwitting, are propagating a form of interpersonal "terrorism?"

All these are interesting questions—and most have found their way into public dialogue. So far, new laws do not resolve which acts will be punished as "terrorism" and which will not. Still, there is room to believe that the definition of a "terrorist" will expand, at least to include those who—as states, organizations, or individuals—"sponsor" (that is, spend or give money to finance) or "harbor" (either actively or passively protect) traditional terrorists and terrorist organizations.

Before discussing "traditional" notions of narcotics and terrorism, let's consider one other related question: Are those who understand the link between drugs and terrorism—whether states, organizations, or individuals—and knowingly continue to fund terrorist organizations through the act of buying drugs—colluding with terrorists? Have you ever thought about it? Do such people, themselves, bear some responsibility for the use of the profits to underwrite terrorist acts? Realistically, how distant must the link between buyer and terrorist be before the narcotics user is free from responsibility for the resulting acts of terrorism? Can responsibility be shed once a buyer understands the link? What if there were *certainty* that funds provided to a drug dealer empowered that dealer—and the organization or chain to which that dealer belongs—to knowingly victimize others and commit acts of traditional terrorism?

Notably, for many Americans this knowledge—precise details on the solid link between drugs and terrorism—is key. In one recent nationwide study, conducted by the Partnership for a Drug-Free America, 59 percent of adolescents said that "knowing the use of illegal drugs supports terrorist activities would make them less likely to use drugs" and 62 percent of parents said that "knowing the use of illegal drugs supports terrorist activities would be helpful to them in talking with their kids about drugs."

Moreover, once the facts were known, "76 percent of parents and 77 percent of teens said they would favor having information about the link between terrorism and illegal drugs delivered by drug education television commercials."[3] Information is empowering, and that may be the best reason to know the details—for those who care about drug use, terrorism, and making well-informed policy and personal decisions. The best place to begin may be a factual overview of terrorism.

WHAT ARE THE MAJOR TERRORIST ORGANIZATIONS?

Within a box one might label "traditional terrorist groups"—that is, groups widely recognized as perpetrators of terrorist acts—there are a number that merit specific mention. Drawing from the secretary of state's list of foreign terrorist organizations (FTOs)[4] and from the "Law Enforcement Guide to Terrorist Groups and Their Known Emblems" (2002),[5] eight organizations jump off the page as incontrovertible, recently active, and deadly terrorist groups: Al Qaeda, Al Jihad, Hamas, Hezbollah, the FARC, the ELN, the PKK, and Shining Path. A short review of who they are, how they operate, and why we should care about them may be a useful starting point.

AL QAEDA AND ITS AFFILIATES

Al Qaeda (spellings vary) means "the base" in Arabic. In some circles, the group is known as the "World Islamic Front for Jihad Against Jews and Crusaders," the "Islamic Army for the Liberation of the Holy Places," the "Usama (or Osama) bin Laden Network," and the "Usama bin Laden Organization."

Responsible for numerous bombings of Western targets over the past two decades, including the horrific events of September 11, 2001, which killed in excess of three thousand innocent people, this group is a loose confederation of anti-Western, pro-Islamic terrorist organizations and cells. The Bush administration has suggested that Al Qaeda may have a presence in some sixty countries. In June 2003, the U.S. government presented an open report to the United Nations Security Council suggesting that there was a "high probability" that Al Qaeda might attempt an attack with a biological, chemical, radioactive, or nuclear weapon in the next two years.[6]

Al Qaeda uses the black Islamic flag of Caliphate, which is the negative image of the white Taliban flag of the former government of Afghanistan.[7] This similarity of imagery is especially important in view of the Taliban government's heavy production of, and intense reliance on, heroin and opium revenues during its pre-2001 regime.

Before the United States–led effort to track down Al Qaeda in Afghanistan and worldwide, the Taliban government controlled Afghanistan's major population centers, including the capital city of Kabul, captured in 1996. During the Taliban's tenure and growing partnership with Al Qaeda, opium and heroin production in Afghanistan increased sharply. Although production was banned in 2001 in order to drive world prices higher, stockpiles were enormous.

Between 1991 and 1999, annual opium production in Afghanistan doubled, from approximately 2,000 to 4,600 tons per year.[8] The impact on the world market for opium and heroin was significant, as was the impact on terrorist funding from Afghan heroin and opium. "[B]y the end of 1999, Afghanistan produced approximately 75 percent of the global supply of opium."[9] These profits were flowing back to the Taliban and its partners. While the Taliban slowed production in 2001,[10] "[b]y the end of 2000 . . . at least 50 percent of heroin consumed in Europe traveled via Central Asia [from Afghanistan]."[11]

Finally, ties between Afghan drug traffickers, terrorists, and regional criminal groups (including those trafficking in human beings, particularly children and women) have also grown tighter over the past decade. "As the drugs trade flourished in Central Asia over the past decade, a number of regional criminal groups—with established relationships with government, law enforcement and military officials—took control of the transportation of drugs from Afghanistan."[12] This has had the added effect of corrupting local and regional law enforcement. For example, "[e]stimates suggest that 50% of law enforcement personnel in Kyrgyzstan [one of the former Soviet republics alone] collaborate with traffickers in one form or another."[13] Referring to heroin, hashish, opium, and marijuana, leading experts suggest that "[t]rafficking these narcotics [from Afghanistan] to external markets . . . remains a priority for many criminal groups."[14]

While U.S. and international pressure on Al Qaeda may be having its effect, a historic link between Afghan heroin and opium on one hand and terrorism on the other is difficult to ignore. The drugs-to-terrorism legacy will be enduring, until an aggressive approach separates, spears, and lands these predators. As Asa Hutchinson, the former director of the federal Drug Enforcement Administration (DEA), noted in 2002:

> [T]he Taliban, which controls opium production and directly taxes the drug trade in Afghanistan, opened its door to Osama Bin Laden and the al Qaeda organization. They built their financial base from heroin trafficking. You see the drugs-to-terror nexus in many different parts of the world. Most Americans now understand that drug money went at least in part to protect the terrorists that attacked American lives. Unless this drugs-terrorism linkage is broken, history is bound to repeat itself.[15]

In fact, Hutchinson's words were prophetic, since recent indications are that heroin trafficking for various illicit purposes is up again in Afghanistan. "With the Taliban defeated [in 2002] and the international community pressuring Afghanistan's new government to launch a comprehensive crackdown on drugs," says one report, "traffickers have been moving huge amounts of heroin out of Afghanistan. . . ."[16] Whether to fund terrorism or for other purposes, another analysis suggests, "Afghanistan has reverted overnight to its role as the Iowa of opium, the raw stuff of heroin."[17] Nowhere, except perhaps in Colombia, has the linkage between the drug trade and terrorism been stronger, historically, than in Afghanistan.

Al Jihad is an Islamic terrorist group associated with Al Qaeda, focusing specifically on attacks against officials of the Egyptian government. This group boasts several thousand "hardcore members" and hundreds of sympathizers, especially in the Cairo area.[18] By way of example, this group is one of many said to have strong ties to Al Qaeda's global network of terrorist organizations.

Others in a loose confederation of terrorist affiliates may include, for example, Filipino groups such as *Abu Sayyaf*, tied to international terrorist Ramzi Yousef,[19] and the New People's Army. More recently, the Filipino Moro Islamic Liberation Front (MILF) seems to have shifted into this category. The MILF was recently tied to a bombing on March 5, 2003, that ranked as the deadliest in Philippines history, wounding 150 and killing 21 at an airport in Davao.[20] Elsewhere, while Al Qaeda affiliations may be difficult to track with certainty, they are supported by strong circumstantial evidence.

HAMAS

Hamas, or the Islamic Resistance Movement—including its military arm, the *Izz Al-Din Al-Qassim* Brigades—is a Palestinian terrorist group noted for suicide bombings that "target . . . Israeli and possibly Western citizens." Published reports indicate that Hamas "receives funding from Palestinian expatriates, Iran and private benefactors in Saudi Arabia."[21] Hamas, which was highly active in 2003, is not confined to terrorist-infested regions of the Middle East.

Three years before the events of 2001, one Middle East expert wrote: "Hamas has developed the largest network of all militant Islamic organizations in the United States," with active components in Texas, Illinois, Missouri, California, New Jersey, Arizona, Oklahoma, Virginia, and New York, adding that Hamas's "conferences . . . have been vehicles to recruit and train terrorists. . . ."[22] Where are these terrorists? Where do they get their revenue? Where will they strike next?

As recently as June 10, 2003, Hamas claimed responsibility for a bombing in Jerusalem that killed two dozen people and injured an additional one hundred persons.[23] Likewise, on March 6, 2003, after a fifty-nine-day lull in the thirty-month-old Palestinian uprising, Hamas claimed responsibility for a suicide bombing that killed fifteen on a bus in northern Israel.[24] Hamas also took responsibility for killing four Israeli soldiers in a tank that hit a land mine on February 15, 2003.[25] The ties between Hamas and narcotics revenue have been a topic of continuing discussion.[26] As indicated below, recent money-laundering indictments strongly implicate Hamas.

HEZBOLLAH

Hezbollah (spellings vary), or the "Party of God," is a Shiite Muslim terrorist organization based in Lebanon. Hezbollah is known for car bombings that target Westerners and Israelis. Published reports indicate that Hezbollah receives financial support from Iran and Islamic groups in the West, including both Europe and North America.[27] There are additional published indications that Hezbollah receives assistance in the form of drug money from diverse locations.[28] Some recent indictments reference Hezbollah directly.

In 1998, testimony before the U.S. Senate suggested that Hezbollah "has kept an unusually low profile in the United States despite an advanced infrastructure of intelligence agents and operatives," with "major centers of support" in Maryland, Michigan, and Illinois, and "hard-core cells" in New Jersey, Texas, Florida, and New York.[29] Hezbollah also has a strong presence in South America, where it may be involved in "arms [trafficking] pipelines running through Brazil and Paraguay to Colombia and Peru."[30] Additionally, "according to law enforcement authorities, the area bordering Paraguay, Argentina, and Brazil—the tri-border area—has become a haven for groups such as Hizballah and HAMAS."[31]

In May 2003 testimony, the DEA observed that "the two major terrorist organizations that exist in the Tri-Border Area of

Paraguay, Argentina, and Brazil are Hizballah and the Islamic Resistance Movement known as HAMAS," adding that "intelligence indicates Islamic fundamentalist terrorist cells operate out of strongholds" in this area; disturbingly, the same testimony apparently indicates that these two groups are using "cocaine trafficking to provide economic assistance to terrorist movements in the Middle East."[32] This assessment was corroborated by the State Department in 2002, which testified that "the Lebanese 'Hizballah' group smuggles cocaine from Latin America to Europe and the Middle East and has in the past smuggled opiates out of Lebanon's Bekaa valley . . . ," adding that "involvement in drug trafficking and other illicit activity may expand as state sponsorship [of Hezbollah terrorism] declines."[33]

Furthermore, according to U.S. senator and former chairman of the U.S. Senate Intelligence Committee Bob Graham (D-FL), "[Hezbollah] has a significant presence of its trained operatives inside the United States waiting for the call to action."[34] This sentiment is corroborated by Deputy Secretary of State Richard Armitage, who has said Hezbollah "may be the A-Team of terrorists. . . ."[35]

THE FARC

The *Fuerzas Armadas Revolucionarias de Colombia* (Revolutionary Armed Forces of Colombia, or FARC) is the largest and most drug money–dependent of South America's terrorist organizations. By most accounts, it is the "best trained and best equipped insurgent organization in Colombia,"[36] with some 8,000 to 25,000 members (estimates vary) and annual revenues between 300 and 600 million U.S. dollars.[37] Terrorist acts have targeted Colombians, Europeans, and Americans, although historically the FARC mainly "conducts armed attacks against Colombian political, economic, military and police targets." Rural targets have included local officials, police stations, and oil pipelines,[38] while urban targets have included government buildings, officials, and civilian activity centers, such as social clubs. Continuing public indications suggest that the FARC, and to a lesser extent, other Colombian terrorist groups, may follow the example of Middle Eastern terrorist groups and intensify attacks on U.S. citizens in Colombia and across the region.

Recent bombings of popular social and political institutions in Bogotá, Colombia's capital, and the FARC execution of Americans aboard a downed light plane in 2003, suggest intensification of the FARC's campaign of terror in cities and against Americans. Additionally, the FARC is notorious for kidnapping members of industrialized cultures; it held a prominent Japanese ransom for $27 million in 2001, kidnapped Germans who were touring rural aid projects, and has kidnapped multiple Americans. The FARC is reported to have extorted hundreds of millions of dollars from local and international businesses over the past several years. Confirming a new anti-American emphasis, the DEA recently reported that the FARC poses a "serious threat" to the security of U.S. citizens living in Colombia. Additionally, DEA indicates the FARC "directly trades cocaine for weapons" and operates on "weapons purchased with cash derived from cocaine sales."[39]

The tight relationship between FARC terrorists and the world's largest drug traffickers, as well as between the FARC and other international terrorist organizations, suggests that cocaine and heroin revenue derived from drugs grown and processed in Colombia contributes directly to global terrorism. Recently, there are indications that the FARC's ties to other terrorist organizations in Europe (including the Irish Republican Army) and the Middle East are tightening.[40] The FARC also enforces discipline within its ranks through terror, for example, kidnapping the families of those who desert FARC ranks. Internationally, Human Rights Watch has reported a series of FARC attacks on civilians and a dramatic increase in murders (numbering in the thousands) through the combined terrorism of the FARC, the ELN, and paramilitary groups (led by *Autodefensas Unidas de Colombia*, or the United Self-Defense Forces of Colombia, or AUC) since 1999.

There are strong indications that FARC terrorist methods

and drug activities are "spilling over" into Mexico, Panama, Venezuela, and Ecuador. Drugs directly involved in the spillover violence include heroin, cocaine, and marijuana, while weapons apprehended to date include caches of AK-47s, Dragonov sniper rifles, and .45-caliber submachine guns.[41]

THE ELN

The *Ejército de Liberación Nacional* (National Liberation Army, or ELN) is another of Colombia's deadly terrorist organizations, similarly focused on instilling terror in Colombia for purposes of destabilizing the regime and deriving substantial revenue from drug-related activities. The ELN is a pro–Communist Cuba, anti-American guerrilla organization that dates to 1965. Today, the group is responsible for regular—at times weekly—assaults on facilities in Colombia involved in oil production and transportation (particularly one oil pipeline), for creating "massive oil spills" through this bombing campaign, and for "extortion" and "bombings against U.S. and other foreign businesses."[42] In some instances, the ELN and the FARC have joined forces to carry out terrorist activities. The ELN derives an estimated 30 percent of its revenue from drugs and drug-related activities.

THE PKK

The *Partiya Karkerên Kurdistanê* (Kurdish Workers' Party, or PKK) is a terrorist organization dedicated to establishing an independent Kurdish state in southeastern Turkey. Cited by the U.S. Department of State as a leading terrorist organization, the PKK primarily targets official security forces in Turkey and Western Europe. To achieve this terrorist aim, it has "bombed tourist sites and hotels" and kidnapped foreign tourists.[43] The PKK is said to be responsible for thousands of civilian deaths and functions in a geography that is rife with drug trafficking. Moreover, one recent State Department report noted that the PKK not only benefits from "taxes" on narcotics trafficking in Europe, but "may be more directly involved in transporting and marketing narcotics in Europe."[44] Similarly, the U.S. Drug Enforcement Administration has testified before Congress that PKK may control a significant portion of the heroin market across Europe, adding that "Turkish press reports state that the PKK produces 60 tons of heroin per year and nets an estimated income of 40 million dollars each year from drug trafficking proceeds."[45]

SHINING PATH

Sendero Luminoso (Shining Path, or SL) is the largest group to terrorize Peru's cities and rural areas. SL operated at a high tempo, with strong anti-Western overtones, throughout the 1980s and 1990s. Described as "among the world's most ruthless guerrilla organizations," its tactics have included bombing rural and urban infrastructure and population centers, as well as the U.S. Embassy in Lima. The group has a membership that has risen and fallen and risen again, oscillating between several thousand and several hundred active members.[46] Funding for its activities has also been traced to Peru's coca-growing areas, which provide raw material used for processed cocaine that, in turn, ends up in the United States.[47] In 2001, there were concrete indications that the SL was "financing [its] operations with profits derived from the drug trade."[48]

OTHER LEADING TERRORIST ORGANIZATIONS

Other leading terrorist organizations include spin-offs from the Palestine Liberation Organization (PLO), a group committed to the formation of an independent state for the displaced Palestinian people—primarily on disputed lands that Israel currently holds or occupies. One of these spin-off groups is the Democratic Front for the Liberation of Palestine (DFLP), which has approximately five hundred members. DFLP has conducted bombings since 1969. Another is the Popular Front for the Liberation of Palestine (PFLP, or the Red Eagle or Halhul Group). This Marxist-Leninist gang of several hundred is both "violently opposed" to the PLO and has attacked Israeli targets through nontraditional means, such as by hot-air balloons and motorized gliders.[49] Significantly, "the Terrorism Research Center has . . . posited the use of PFLP infrastructure in Lebanon for drug transfers."[50]

Several other terrorist organizations are suspected of links to the narcotics trade. These include:

- Palestine Islamic Jihad (the PIJ), which is committed to founding an Islamic Palestinian state, destroying Israel, and opposing moderate Arab governments;
- *Gama'a al-Islamiyya*, or the Islamic Group, an "Egyptian extremist movement" that has a reported presence in California, Maryland, North Carolina, New Jersey, and Massachusetts;[51]
- the *Mujahedin-e Khalq* Organization (the MEK or MKO), which has sponsored terrorist acts against the Iranian government, including attacks on thirteen Iranian embassies worldwide;
- *Aum Shinrikyo*, also known as Aum Supreme Truth, which dates to 1987, claims nine thousand members, aims to "take over Japan and then the world," and in 1995, released sarin nerve gas in Tokyo train stations;
- the Liberation Tigers of Tamil Eelam (LTTE), the most violent terrorist group in Sri Lanka, which has one thousand members and a string of assassinations and bombings attached to its name;[52]
- the *Autodefensas Unidas de Colombia* (the United Self-Defense Forces of Colombia, or the AUC), a violent paramilitary organization in Colombia responsible for civilian massacres that appear to have been a response to terrorist acts by the FARC and ELN during the 1990s;[53]

- the *Kahane Chai* (KACH), which targets Arabs, Palestinians, and official Israelis who do not accept the aim of restoring "the biblical state of Israel" and reportedly has members or sympathizers in America and Europe;[54]
- the Islamic Movement of Uzbekistan (IMU), which "reportedly profited from the drug trade out of Afghanistan and trafficking through Central Asia to Russia and Europe;"[55]
- the Basque Fatherland and Liberty (ETA), which 2002 testimony by the State Department notes was "involved in a variety of crimes from drug trafficking to money laundering;"[56] and
- generally, Russian Organized Crime (ROC) groups, which recent DEA testimony suggests "are forming alliances with criminal entities such as . . . Mexican and Colombian drug trafficking groups . . .[and] increasingly facilitate drug shipments in Latin America and Asia to the United States and Europe, and are involved in weapons-for-drugs shipments."[57]

Finally, there are more shadowy groups that are not listed as terrorists, but that swim in the same brackish pond. One of these is *Hizb Al-Ikhwan Al-Muslimoon* (the Muslim Brotherhood Movement), formed in 1928. This group claims branches or cells in seventy countries. One affiliate is the Muslim Arab Youth Association, an organization reportedly weighted with "militant" Egyptians and Palestinians, allegedly sponsoring annual conferences that have included "terrorist training sessions," and purportedly possessing ties to Oklahoma, Arizona, California, Michigan, New Jersey, Illinois, Texas, and Missouri. Another affiliate, the American Muslim Council (AMC) is reported to be the "de facto lobbying arm of the Muslim Brotherhood in the United States."[58] Last, *Fatah* (the Movement for the National Liberation of Palestine) claims between six thousand and eight thousand members. In the past, Fatah has reportedly carried out terrorist attacks in twenty countries, including the United States, injuring some nine hundred persons.[59]

The impact of terrorism on foreign soil should not be underestimated. Where terrorist organizations flourish, the cost in human life is intolerably high. In Colombia, for example, the DEA estimates that the FARC, ELN, and AUC were collectively responsible for 3,500 murders in 2002, and the people of that country suffered more kidnappings than any other nation. Not surprisingly, members of the FARC and AUC were indicted by the U.S. Justice Department in 2002 on narcotics and terrorism charges.[60]

Before discussing in detail the links between narcotics and some of these terrorist organizations, readers are invited to think—first—about the role of illegal narcotics in the United States. The next chapter discusses the implications for national security of a different phenomenon—Americans' addiction to illegal narcotics.

3

The American Addiction

Who uses all these illegal narcotics? What illegal narcotics are most commonly available in the United States? Where do dangerous narcotics really come from? What costs do they impose on us—as individuals, communities, and a nation? Aside from funding terrorist organizations, what other palpable dangers do narcotics pose? Such questions give context to the larger discussion about drug-funded terrorism.

Similarly, understanding the ruthless, predatory underworld of drug trafficking helps us understand its relationship to terrorism. How do drug trafficking organizations work? What motivations underlie drug trafficking? How do these motivations differ from those that underlie terrorism? Is there a shared indifference to human life inherent in all such organizations? Are there common elements driving these two types of organizations together?

At the outset, it is important to see the profile of drug abuse in America accurately—not as Hollywood or naysayers portray it, but as it really is. Most young people do *not* use drugs, although there have been discouraging trends over the past decade that reveal slippage in long-held attitudes and behaviors. These trends suggest either a growing lack of information about the dangers inherent in particular drugs or a growing tendency to ignore information about the dangers of drug use. This may be attributable to a general increase in risky behaviors;

confusion about scientific facts; the wider availability of narcotics; higher narcotic purity levels for heroin, cocaine, methamphetamine, and marijuana, each of which can trigger addiction; the appearance of new drug labels, types, and brands; lower narcotics prices; conflicting messages in the media about drug dangers; and efforts by a vocal minority to legalize narcotics for wider overall use.

Regardless of causes, the United States struggles with a national problem that borders on epidemic among certain age groups. While teen drug use declined in 2002, decade-long trends remain disturbing. Sadly, this problem is bound to have long-term medical, economic, political, and cultural effects beyond the implications of funding terrorism.

AMERICANS' USE OF NARCOTICS

In general, narcotics use and addiction are driven by drug availability, purity, price, and cultural norms. Use and addiction are also driven by the level, type, quality, and availability of accurate information on drug dangers, as well as the means for preventing or avoiding drug abuse and addiction. What we *don't* know *can* hurt us and often *does*. Generally, "teenagers are considering the information in [science-based education] messages before deciding whether or not to use drugs, and they are making better decisions," according to one leading study in 2002. That same study, *Monitoring the Future*, noted, "teenagers are increasingly choosing not to use marijuana [and] not to use ecstasy and other club drugs. . . ."[1] However, overall abuse numbers remain disturbingly high, especially for younger Americans.

An overview of leading data on the role of narcotics in the United States, and the direct dangers posed by narcotics, is important. Solid numbers illustrate how America wrestles with addiction, together with the direct and indirect effects of addiction on revenue streams—including those to terrorist organizations. Although virtually *any* narcotic can be used to illustrate this point, heroin, which has recently reemerged in a pure form and has strong connections to Afghanistan and Colombia, provides a timely example.

One of the most persuasive sets of data is offered by examining heroin availability, purity, and use against the backdrop of health consequences in the United States in the 1980s and 1990s. Specifically, according to the DEA, the rise in average purity recorded by the DEA during the 1980s and early 1990s corresponded directly to increased availability of high-purity Colombian and Southeast Asian heroin and, to a lesser extent, increases in the purity of Mexican heroin. Thus, in 1998, the average purity of South American samples obtained through the DEA was at a historical high point. So, what does that mean? It means that more heroin was coming into the United States, in turn forcing prices down and regional purities up. "By selling at high purity and a low price, [Colombian drug lords] saw they could make inroads into the market share held by the Asian countries."[2] At the same time, whereas unusually pure South American heroin accounted for 75 percent of the total heroin analyzed by the DEA in 1997, overall heroin use and addiction were climbing.

Doesn't that make sense? Consider the heroin trap—physical and psychological quicksand—into which some young Americans have recently stepped. Statistics support the argument that higher availability of this addictive drug leads to higher rates of use across studied populations, which in turn produces higher rates of addiction and negative health consequences. This principle applies to all narcotics, although some trigger addiction more quickly or produce irreversible health effects before addiction. In the 1980s and 1990s, falling prices for heroin induced more use and buying. At the same time, increases in purity trapped more people in addiction. As a result, overall use of the drug rose—and with it emergency-room visits and breadth of addiction.

Not surprisingly, by 1997, data from the National Household Survey on Drug Abuse revealed that "heroin use has increased steadily since 1992" and "the number of Americans who used heroin in the past month increased from 68,000 . . . in 1993 to 325,000 . . . in 1997."[3]

What effects did increased heroin use and addiction have—beyond putting substantially more money in the coffers of traffickers and terrorists? As availability and purity of heroin have risen, wider use and addiction have followed. But these have not been the only effects. A variety of negative health effects have been recorded.

According to the annual *Drug Abuse Warning Network* (*DAWN*), which chronicles emergency-room incidents in hospitals across the United States, "the annual number of heroin-related emergency room (ER) mentions increased from 42,000 in 1989 to 76,000 in 1995—an 80-percent increase. . . ."[4] This number, which embodies a range of medical issues, continues to rise.

Of course, this should come as no surprise, either. Research indicates that on top of their addictive properties, heroin and cocaine have other unexpected, acute, and undesirable effects. The same is true for Ecstasy (also known as "E" or "butterfly"), GHB, PCP, LSD, Oxycontin, Vicodin, and marijuana at various levels of purity, as well as methamphetamine and other drugs of abuse, such as inhalants, prescription stimulants, and depressants.[5] Thus, "[a]cute myocardial infarction is the most commonly reported consequence of cocaine misuse, usually occurring in men who are young, fit and healthy and who have minimal, if any, risk factors for cardiovascular disease."[6] Likewise, acute effects are registered across a panoply of narcotics, ranging from brain damage (common with Ecstasy and inhalant abuse) to reproductive organ damage and reduced immune function (traceable to use of THC and opiates).[7]

What does all this tell us? One clear message is that a substantial number of Americans have a narcotics dependence problem, which tends to make narcotics revenue a reliable source of income for those who would prey on unwitting, risk-taking, and addicted persons.

Medically, the phenomenon or trap of addiction may—in a way—explain the growing role of narcotics in American society. For example, even minimal repeated exposure to opioid drugs "induces the brain mechanisms of dependence, which leads to daily drug use to avert the unpleasant symptoms of drug withdraw," after which "prolonged use produces more long-lasting changes in the brain that may underlie the compulsive drug-seeking process of decision-making, and related adverse consequences that are the hallmarks of addiction."[8] Other research demonstrates that "drugs' effects on dopamine levels and function [in the brain] are a key to the motivation for abuse."[9] In short, use can trigger brain function changes that, in turn, create unexpected and enduring addiction.

AMERICAN NARCOTICS DEPENDENCE—THE BIGGER PICTURE

Moving from individual and drug-specific problems to the "big picture," other hard data demonstrate the complex relationship between American society and illegal narcotics. In 2000, driven by first-time users, national statistics suddenly showed "[d]rug related deaths reached a record level . . . , while users have been able to buy cocaine and heroin at some of the lowest prices in decades. . . ."[10] But that is not the whole story.

Encouragingly, narcotics have *not* typically featured so prominently in our nation's culture. In fact, between the mid-1980s and 1992, prices for most dangerous narcotics (including heroin, cocaine, and marijuana) rose through a coordinated effort to reduce the incoming supply of narcotics, and an increase in federal, state, and local law enforcement. At the same time, hard-hitting, well-targeted prevention messages for youth—presented by the Partnership for a Drug-Free America, parents, and nationwide civic organizations—proved pervasive and persuasive.

Again, not surprisingly, efforts to educate and confiscate produced lower initiation rates—Americans recognized that narcotics were a dead-end street, no matter *where* the money went. "Monthly cocaine use dropped from nearly 3 million users in

1988 to 1.3 million in 1990. . . . Between 1991 and 1992, overall drug abuse dropped from 14.5 million users to 11.4 million."[11] Americans had the data and the ability to protect their health and future. With accurate information, as a group, Americans worked to get out of the use and addiction traps.

Looked at from another angle, when prices rose, "[o]verall casual drug use by Americans dropped by more than half [between 1977 and 1992]. . . . Between 1985 and 1992 alone, monthly cocaine use declined by 78 percent."[12] That was good news for Americans. It also meant that revenues from narcotics fell for those producing and distributing them.

The double effect for the United States was better health and fewer drug-funded criminal enterprises. One expert noted, "crack-cocaine use sharply declined from nearly half a million in 1990 to just over 300,000 two years later in 1992," and "in virtually every category of illegal drug, we saw sharp declines" from the mid-1980s through 1992, including "an astonishing 61 percent decline" of regular marijuana users between 1985 and 1992.[13] The point: Narcotics dependency—for an individual or society—*can* be reduced. Once recognized as a threat to our health and safety, actions can be taken to turn back narcotics use, addiction, and the secondary effects of funding criminal and terrorist enterprises with drug proceeds.

Effective education and leadership under President Ronald Reagan and First Lady Nancy Reagan made a substantial difference by reducing drug use and drug revenues to traffickers. This effort was extended by President George H.W. Bush. Together, Presidents Reagan and Bush saw the menace presented by narcotics and terrorism, and reenergized the nation's counternarcotics and counterterrorism efforts. These presidents were assisted by numerous leaders in the U.S. Congress, drawn from both political parties. Clearly, the 2002 data suggest that the same can be done again.

4

The Links Between Drugs and Terrorism

According to the White House Office of National Drug Control Policy, "about half of the 28 organizations identified as terrorist by the U.S. State Department are funded by sales of illegal drugs."[1] While this fact is arresting, details are the key to understanding the nature of that relationship.

Leading questions addressed in this chapter are these: What geographic, political, and financial links bind drug traffickers and terrorist groups? Do drug-trafficking and terrorist group memberships overlap, and if so, how much? Are drug traffickers and terrorists also tied to international criminal organizations that deal in arms, people, and other contraband? Do terrorists and drug traffickers reinforce one another? If so, how?

To tackle these questions, a look at geography—some of the "hot spots" of terrorism and drug trafficking—will help. Several hot spots are commonly cited:

- Afghanistan, Pakistan, the Balkans, and the Central Asian republics are home to concentrations of Al Qaeda terrorists and massive heroin production;[2]
- Colombia, Peru, and Bolivia are home to the FARC, the ELN, and AUC terrorists, as well as massive cocaine and heroin production; and

- Mexico and the United States are home to pseudo-ephedrine and methamphetamine, marijuana, and heroin production, as well as networks financing terrorism.

It is hard to find a clearer example than Afghanistan of the Gordian knot binding terrorists to narcotics traffickers—unless Colombia provides such a case. As an example of terrorism fattened on narcotics revenue, Afghanistan has textbook simplicity. Historical context is helpful.

THE HISTORICAL CONTEXT

Although Marxist-Leninist, Islamic and liberation terrorists, drug traffickers, and generic international criminals have long crossed paths, the breakup of the Soviet Union in the late 1980s was a seminal event.

That one event changed the world's balance of power in ways that far exceeded the end of "containment theory"—a theory by which the United States and Western Europe strived to limit Soviet expansion to boundaries agreed after World War II.

Beyond ending the delicate equilibrium between West and East, the Soviet Union's fall brought an abrupt end to Soviet care and feeding of insurgency movements—often led by terrorists—around the world. Smaller states had to fend for themselves now, and terrorist organizations once flush with Soviet money for sowing instability found themselves beached on the sands of an unsettling "New World Order."

During the 1990s, this erosion of direct and indirect support for international terrorism by "state sponsors" caused terrorist organizations to reach for other means of financing.[3] State Department officials recently described the evolution: "In the past, state sponsors provided funding for terrorists, and their relationships with terrorist organizations were used to secure territory or provide access to gray arms networks. . . . Lately, however, as state sponsorship of terrorism has come under increased scrutiny and greater international condemnation, terrorist groups have looked increasingly at drug trafficking as a source of revenue."[4] This 2002 testimony included a telling kicker: "[Drug] trafficking often has a two-fold purpose for the terrorists. . . . Not only does it provide funds, it also furthers the strategic objectives of the terrorists. . . . Some terrorist groups believe that they can weaken their enemies by flooding their societies with addictive drugs."[5]

Though terrorist groups do not rely exclusively on narcotics for funding, the attraction of feeding on an addicted population for steady revenue has had powerful appeal. The less an addicted population realizes the link to its own general welfare, the easier the feeding process is. Many terrorist groups—from the Middle East to South America—began to ratchet up their reliance on drug profits. That said, the shift encompassed terrorist groups of many types, drew revenue from many geographic areas, and often bridged the worlds of legitimate and illegitimate business activities. As one commentator noted:

> The best example of such a shift [away from state sponsorship] was the Provisional IRA's large-scale 1980s move into the crime arena. While historically being involved in minor protection-racket activities, as the Cold War drew to an end, the Provisional IRA became more involved in illicit gambling, running gaming arcades, taxi firms, and even drug running. This diversification was simply a more sophisticated version of a slide into less than politically "pure" activities mirrored elsewhere, most often in Latin America.[6]

Even low-tech terrorism requires funding for certain basics, such as weapons; recruitment, including abductions; training, including methods of brainwashing in the "art of fanaticism;" attack planning; materiel, from equipment for surveillance to bomb-making ingredients; information on targets and people; and living arrangements over time. After the depletion of Soviet funding, then, terrorist groups felt a growing need for reliable and lucrative sources of income. One fact on which leading writers about terrorism tend to agree is that, whatever its objectives and means, "carrying out terrorist activities costs money."[7]

As long as the Western appetite for narcotics continues, and as long as Westerners—in Europe and the United States—see no major geopolitical consequences flowing from their continued dependence on narcotics, the reservoir will remain deep. In short, narcotics offer a steady source of financing to terrorist organizations. Even if selected governments legalize some or all dangerous narcotics, the ability to pump highly pure drugs into these countries at low prices, particularly to the youth, will continue—unless otherwise addressed.

By way of example, the Taliban government—and its terrorist allies, such as Al Qaeda—benefited directly from cultivating, transporting, and selling heroin and opium in unprecedented quantities to Europe. By 2001, one leading expert on terrorism reported that "[a] lucrative drug market and a desirable standard of living has ensured that Western Europe remains an important destination for [Afghanistan's] illicit narcotics. . . ."[8]

In fact, Al Qaeda's choice of Afghanistan as a base of operations may not have been driven solely by its isolation and harsh topography. Even before the attacks of September 11, strong indications supported the link between Middle Eastern narcotics trafficking and Middle Eastern terrorism—both resident in Afghanistan. For example, Vitaly Naumkin, president of the Center for Strategic and Political Studies in Moscow, noted in 2001 that "Russia has been warning for years of the emergence of an interconnected network of drug-funded Islamic extremists who carry terrorism to unseen heights."[9]

Afghanistan may have been specially suited to facilitating the link between narcotics and a network for widening international terror. Notably, Afghanistan represented the introduction of an extremist Islamic ideology promoting terrorism into a non-Arab country, creating a new and relatively remote base from which to project terrorism. One expert noted in 2001: "Several thousands of Arabs in Afghanistan, like bin Laden, have become enormously influential and are the main force radicalizing the Taliban . . . [and] are injecting their global terrorist agenda into what was formerly a local Islamic extremist movement."[10]

Strangely, there are some indications that South America could represent a future hotbed for such a volatile combination. One public account, in June 2003, noted that a top private intelligence company had issued a report on the topic:

> While calling attention towards the possibility of an Al Qaeda attack in Latin America—it is a zone where the United States does not expect an attack and where there are plenty of US targets—the report reminds readers that the terrorist organization has strong ties to a large number of Hezbollah members in the tri-border area of Brazil, Argentina, and Paraguay.

Moreover, the June 2003 account notes a "surprising piece of data," namely "that the report stated factually that Hezbollah and the FARC, the Colombian guerrilla group, have been in the business of swapping guns for drugs for some time now."[11] Accordingly, Afghanistan's seemingly special conditions for fomenting an international, drug-funded terrorism base may not, after all, be unique.

In Afghanistan, widespread opium cultivation was the rule in the late 1990s, until the Taliban had stockpiled large quantities of heroin. In 2001, the Taliban imposed a ban on cultivation and manipulated the world heroin market to create higher prices, particularly in Europe. Since the Taliban's fall, expansive cultivation has again become the rule. As long as consumption remains high, there is every reason to believe that the leading recipients of drug revenue will include Afghan warlords, corrupt governments, and those who promote terrorism.

Looking back, the production of opium in Afghanistan has risen sharply since the breakup of the Soviet Union. Absent sustained international pressure to cut this production, together with credible efforts to seed alternative income sources—or dramatically reduce consumption in Europe and America—heroin production in Afghanistan will remain high.

Over the past decade and a half, tell-tale trend lines have become clear: According to United Nations (UN) statistics, the production of opium in Afghanistan grew steadily beginning in 1988. Between 1988 and 1991, it increased 100 percent. Between 1991 and 1999, production grew from an estimated 2,000 tons to a record 4,600 tons. By the end of 1999, Afghanistan produced approximately 75 percent of the global supply of opium.[12]

RECENT EVIDENCE OF THE NARCOTICS–TERROR LINK

New trend lines are emerging today. These trends further support a connection between drug money and terrorism, even post-9/11. These trend lines span the globe, from America to Russia. In fact, Russian President Vladimir Putin recently remarked, "terrorism and drugs are absolutely related phenomena. . . . They share the same roots, and, it seems, the same destructive force."[13]

Moreover, legal cases and other evidence filling in the connection are persuasive. According to Steven Casteel, assistant administrator for intelligence at DEA, "Philosophically, we need to be concerned about the drug issue because it is so closely tied to terrorism. . . . since state-sponsored terrorism began to decline in the 1980's, the DEA has seen terrorist groups across the world—include al-Qaida—turn to drugs to help fund their activities."[14]

In January 2003, several men were arrested in connection with narcotics trafficking for the specific purpose of purchasing weapons for Al Qaeda terrorists. The drugs being sold to support terrorism were heroin and hashish. One riveting account offered these details:

> Three men accused of trying to acquire anti-aircraft missiles for the Al Qaeda terrorist network have dropped their fight against extradition to the United States [from Hong Kong]. . . . [The two Pakistanis and an American of Indian descent] were arrested by local police after offering a large stash of heroin and hashish to undercover FBI agents as barter for the four sophisticated shoulder-launched missiles destined for Al Qaeda, according to the Hong Kong Government.[15]

Equally disturbing, the origins of this transaction may have been in the United States. According to one contemporaneous report, "this is the first time a significant Al Qaeda connection has cropped up in Hong Kong. . . . But indications are [that] the illicit transaction—involving 600 kilograms of heroin and five tons of hashish—was conceived in California."[16]

Likewise, in February 2003, criminal charges were brought against a Canadian contraband trafficker who appeared to have been funneling the proceeds back to Hezbollah.[17] According to news accounts, "the indictment alleges that Hezbollah sheiks in Lebanon and Iran were involved," and the accused "made 'numerous' trips overseas to commit acts of fraud," "conspired with at least two individuals with strong ties to Hezbollah," and "would, on occasion, telephone sheiks in Lebanon and Iran to clear criminal acts he was committing." A Canadian account further adds that "Hezbollah established a major presence in Canada throughout the 1990s and used the country to raise money, purchase materiel and hide operatives before and after attacks."[18]

TRACING THE MONEY AND VERIFYING THE LINKAGE

Tracing money flows is another way of verifying terrorism's reliance upon drug money for its operations. Today, there is new evidence of that connection—through Al Qaeda and others—even in the period after September 11.

According to the U.S. State Department,

> the U.S. campaign against global terrorism in 2002 highlighted the importance of international drug control programs . . . [and] [a]s the single greatest source of illegal revenue, the drug trade has long been the mainstay of violent political insurgencies, rogue regimes, international criminal organizations and terrorists of every stripe. [19]

One leading effort in tracing money flows is represented by the U.S. Customs Service's so-called "Operation Green Quest," a multiagency task force involving some 240 agents and 460 analysts. This operation's aim is to track the flow of money backward, to the sources from which terrorists first get funding, and cut them off. Reports of the operation suggest that "as terrorist financiers are forced out of the banking system [by worldwide pressure and cooperation], they are turning to riskier ways to move money, including smuggling cash . . . and drugs." [20]

U.S. Customs Commissioner Bob Bonner describes his mission as, "staunching the flow of funds to international terrorist organizations like the al-Qaida, depriving them of the financial wherewithal to mount and stage major terrorist attacks against the United States and the American People and frankly elsewhere in the world." [21]

Since being established in 2001, Operation Green Quest's work has "resulted in 79 arrests, 70 indictments and 600 open investigations," according to the U.S. Customs Service. There was no immediate breakout of drug- and non-drug-related cases. However, in one possible indication of drug-derived revenue, "Operation Green Quest has seized nearly $333 million—of which $21 million constituted smuggled currency and monetary instruments seized at the Nation's border."[22]

Not surprisingly, the DEA has also recently conducted a number of operations to trace where drug money goes. Several of the most striking were Operation Caribe, Operation Juno, Operation White Terror, Operation Mountain Express III, and Operation Containment. With 79 offices in 58 countries, the DEA is able to conduct widespread international activities, often assisting other agencies' investigations. During Operations Caribe and Juno, Colombian cocaine money was traced to sophisticated money-laundering operations. In Operation White Terror, DEA and FBI investigators thwarted a Colombian-based, drugs-for-weapons organization, producing charges of "material assistance to a terrorist organization"; the weapons intercepted included automatic rifles, grenades, and rocket grenades. In the fourth operation, Mountain Express III, more than one hundred individuals in twelve cities across Canada and the United States were apprehended and prosecuted for trafficking 26 tons of pseudoephedrine, an amount sufficient for making 50,000 pounds of methamphetamine. Finally, in 2002's Operation Containment, the DEA coordinated a number of countries in a major, post-Taliban heroin interception effort. This effort was intended "to deprive international terrorist groups of the financial basis for their activities . . . ," and sought to "seize as much Southwest Asian heroin as possible before it reached the lucrative markets of Western Europe and the United States." In total, the operation netted more then 1,700 kilograms of heroin, "with an estimated value between $28 and $51 million."[23]

Plainly, as these operations suggest, tracing the money used by terrorist organizations back to drug trafficking is one way to illustrate the link. Another is case-by-case review.

MONEY, TERRORISM, NARCOTICS, AND IRAQ

One indication of the breadth of possible drug funding for terror emerged, again out of Operation Green Quest, in December

2002. In late 2002, indictments were issued for eleven people in five countries. These people were indicted for international smuggling and money laundering. Their illegal activities funneled roughly $28 million in U.S. money and goods to Iraq illegally over a period of thirty months.

Arrest warrants were served in the United States, and also in the United Kingdom, Jordan, Dubai, and Iraq. "Officials wouldn't say whether the money was raised through individual contributions or illicit activities like drug trafficking," though the sums were sizable.[24] Those arrested in the United States are "accused of funding Hamas, a militant Islamist group based in the Middle East."[25] Whether Iraq in 2002 was deeply entangled with drug money is uncertain. What is beyond doubt is that Saddam Hussein's Iraq was involved directly in both an internal regime of terror and wider international terrorism. The Council on Foreign Relations has explained the scope of Iraq's terror links: "Saddam Hussein's dictatorship provided headquarters, operating bases, training camps, and other support to terrorist groups fighting the governments of neighboring Turkey and Iran, as well as to hard-line Palestinian groups." Moreover, "[d]uring the 1991 Gulf War, Saddam commissioned several failed terrorist attacks on U.S. facilities," and "[t]he State Department lists Iraq as a state sponsor of terrorism."[26]

5

Drugs and Terror at Home: North and South America

Drug terrorism and regional stability are also closely linked in North and South America. Like Afghanistan, Iraq, and points east, Colombia—to our south—is pivotal to understanding the link between narcotics and terrorism. So direct is the link between drugs and terrorism in Colombia that Secretary of State Colin Powell, in December 2002, spoke of U.S. support to Colombia in these terms: "Today, Colombia is engaged in its own war against terrorism and the narco-trafficking that funds it. The U.S. stands with the people of Colombia in this struggle."[1] On the strength of leadership from Secretary Colin Powell, House Speaker J. Dennis Hastert, Attorney General John Ashcroft, and others in the Bush administration, America's stand with the people of Colombia against terrorism has been increasingly real. Colombia is an important starting point for understanding the linkage in North and South America.

INDICTMENTS IN 2002 LINK NARCOTICS AND TERRORISM

In November 2002, Attorney General John Ashcroft, flanked by FBI Director Robert Mueller, DEA Administrator Asa Hutchinson, White House "drug czar" John Walters, and other Justice Department officials, handed down indictments of Colombia's FARC terrorists. The attorney general explained these indictments as follows:

> Today marks another significant milestone in the war against terrorism and drug trafficking in the Americas. In three separate indictments, leaders of the Revolutionary Armed Forces of Colombia, known by the Spanish language acronym FARC, stand charged with hostage-taking and drug trafficking in order to obtain money and weapons for terrorist activities.[2]

The attorney general noted that the FARC has been designated a "foreign terrorist organization" by the U.S. State Department since 1977. These indictments contained murder charges involving specific civilians, as well as other criminal counts, including "conspiracy to commit hostage-taking resulting in death, hostage-taking resulting in death, hostage-taking and using a firearm during a crime of violence."[3]

To these charges must be added the U.S. indictment of FARC leaders in March 2002, charging them with "trafficking cocaine into the United States and exchanging cocaine for weapons and material that support the FARC's [terrorist] activities."[4] Finally, an April 2002 indictment sets forth additional facts "charging the FARC and leaders of the FARC with conspiring to target, surveil, abduct and murder three Americans." On the occasion of the November 2002 indictment, Attorney General Ashcroft added a scathing summation of his own: "The State Department has called the FARC the most dangerous international terrorist organization based in the Western Hemisphere. And our indictments show them as terrorists, drug traffickers, kidnappers and murderers."[5]

Explaining the basis for this linkage and the criminal charges, Attorney General Ashcroft presented a number of new facts. He emphasized that this "drug indictment is a result of an ongoing two-year investigation of narcotics trafficking by FARC conducted by DEA in cooperation with the governments of Colombia, Suriname and Brazil. . . ."

Last, the attorney general offered praise to the government

of Colombia and to the deputy attorney general, whom he noted "has had a commitment to fight the scourge of drugs in America, intensified by the awareness of the narcotics and terrorism nexus, which is especially threatening."[6]

Citing evidence of the relationship between the FARC's terrorist activities in Colombia and direct involvement in drug trafficking to the United States, former DEA Administrator Asa Hutchinson, now undersecretary of the Homeland Security Department, spoke of bringing the FARC to justice:

> Clearly, these indictments . . . reflect that both guns and drugs were used as weapons against the United States and citizens of the United States. . . . These indictments are an essential step in assuring the survival of democracy and the rule of law in Colombia. It is our hope that bringing the terrorist leaders to justice will diminish violence, will bring stability and peace to Colombia, as well as supporting the rule of law and the charges that have been brought against them in the United States.[7]

DRUG CZAR SHINES AN UNCOMFORTABLE LIGHT

Little more needed to be said about the FARC. And so, White House "drug czar" John Walters shined an uncomfortably bright light on another aspect of the drug-terrorism connection, implications for everyday Americans. His main point was hard to miss. Referring to these indictments, he pointedly observed:

> [T]his is also a reminder once again that American consumers are the single largest funders of anti-democratic forces in the hemisphere. As the President has said, that fact is intolerable. And the results of the American drug consumer are reminders every day in the countries of this hemisphere where law enforcement officials, judges, political officials,

> innocent civilians, Americans among them, are terrorized, murdered and made victim of the drug trade. . . . The fact is, if you use drugs, stop. It's not only good for you, it's good for your community, it's good for your country.[8]

Walters then added a layer that most Americans do not often think about. Suggesting that individual responsibility for national security rests with every American, he tied personal behavior to the drugs-terrorism connection:

> [M]ore importantly, if you know somebody who [uses illegal drugs], this is not a responsible stand—to look the other way. Minding your business means urging those people to stop doing what is not only harming them and those around them, but harming the principles of democracy and justice in this hemisphere and throughout the world. You have a responsibility, not only as a user but as a bystander, to be a force for reducing this problem. . . . Until we do that, on both the demand and supply sides, we cannot be happy with where we are.[9]

THE COLOMBIA SITUATION IN CONTEXT

Exhaustive evidence backs up these administration assessments of the tight connection between narcotics and terrorism in Colombia. Similar evidence supports a resurgence of drug-related terrorism in Peru, Venezuela, Bolivia, and elsewhere in the region.[10] Recent evidence also supports the specific connection between "groups with links to terrorist organizations" and narcotics trafficking in Paraguay and Brazil. One expert reported in 2003, for example, that Paraguay "is home to thousands of individuals of Arabic descent who have taken advantage of Paraguay's relaxed immigration laws. . . . DEA intelligence has revealed that some of these individuals are utilizing the proceeds from cocaine trafficking to provide economic assistance to terrorist movements in the Middle East."[11]

Specific instances mark Colombian terrorism as a growing threat to the region and to Americans. Consider a few examples:

- In February 2003, after a small plane with U.S. citizens aboard crashed in Colombia's Caqueta region, the FARC claimed credit for shooting it down, executed two people aboard (one American citizen and one Colombian), and kidnapped three American citizens, threatening to kill all three if any rescue attempt were undertaken.

- Referring to FARC terrorism, congressional hearings in 2002 noted that "in the past decade, 5,000 Colombian police have been killed, thousands of civilians slaughtered, and the government's authority obliterated in much of the country," adding that "the FARC has already declared the U.S. to be an enemy, terming U.S. assistance to the Colombian government an 'act of war.'"[12] *The Wall Street Journal* argued in 1998 that "more than 4,000 Colombian police officers have died at the hands of narco-traffickers."[13]

- Congressional concern surrounding the narcotics-terrorism nexus in Colombia crystallized in 2001: "Should Colombia be fatally undermined, the contagion would spread to neighboring countries and beyond. . . . [Already,] Americans in Colombia are routinely kidnapped and even murdered," wrote Congress. Moreover, "the FARC's promotion of an increasing supply of drugs to the United States guarantees an ever-more-deadly impact here at home."[14] A State Department travel warning issued early in 2003 noted that "in the past three years, 26 Americans were reported kidnapped in various parts of the country."[15]

- Extensive clashes between the FARC and the Colombian Army continued throughout 2002 and 2003 as the Colombian government sought to track FARC terrorists and find kidnap victims, especially in the coca-producing areas of Caqueta and Putumayo, near Colombia's southern border with Ecuador.[16]

Of equal concern is a growing relationship between Colombian terrorists and the global terrorism network, including terrorist organizations in Europe and the Middle East. Consider new data points:

- In February 2003, former FARC members testified in a Colombia-based trial of three Irish citizens. The three were indicted as members of the Irish Republican Army (IRA) terrorist group on charges that the IRA is now training the FARC in IRA terrorist techniques.[17]

- Congressional hearings and other accounts identify a new relationship between the FARC and European terrorist groups, ranging from the IRA to the Basque terrorist group *Euskadi Ta Askatasuna* (Basque Homeland and Freedom, or ETA).[18] For example, hearings in 2002 concluded, "the available evidence strongly indicates that involvement of the IRA in Colombia extends beyond the three members who were captured and that [the IRA] has had a presence in that country for at least 3 years."[19]

- Congressional investigators have zeroed in on drug financing in Colombia as one method of promoting and sustaining terrorism. Speaking to this point in 2002, the chairman of the U.S. House International Relations Committee noted: "One of the most disturbing developments is the [emergent] nexus of organized crime, terrorism and drugs. Nowhere is this destructive combination more advanced than in Colombia."[20]

- At the same time, Colombian terrorists' reliance on drug money triggers other concerns: "Events in Colombia make it clear that global terrorist networks are interchangeable, aggressive, and know no boundaries or borders, threatening anyone and any nation," and "the situation in Colombia illustrates the growing phenomenon of proceeds from illicit drugs playing a major role in financing the activities of global terrorist networks,"[21] according to leading experts.

Lest there be any doubt, a direct, sad, and incontrovertible tie binds North American drug users to Colombia's terrorism, instability, and record murder rate. The instability in Colombia grows out of the rise in drug-funded terrorism. Illicit drug money flows back to Colombia's terrorists and murderers from consumers in North America. More specifically, most of that money can be traced to Americans who buy cocaine, heroin, and marijuana from trafficking organizations that originate in Colombia and Mexico. Specifically:

- Law enforcement and congressional authorities say, "Colombia produces 90 percent of the cocaine and at least 70 percent of the heroin sold in the United States," explaining a more direct basis upon which "the U.S. has a significant presence in that country to assist the Colombian authorities in fighting that threat."[22]

- The DEA recently synthesized the narcotics-terrorism link in a December 2001 symposium entitled "Target America: Traffickers, Terrorists and Your Kids," prior to which DEA noted: "What few Americans realize . . . is the inexorable and historical links between the activities of terrorists and those of narcotics traffickers around the world."[23]

- In April 2002, DEA Administrator Asa Hutchinson focused new attention on Colombia, explaining that the Bush administration "increasingly sees links between terrorism and drug-trafficking money."[24]

Finally, the proximity and enormity of the threat posed by Colombia's instability to the region and to everyday Americans is easy to underestimate:

- On February 11, 2003, in an open hearing before the U.S. Senate Intelligence Committee entitled "Current and Projected National Security Threats to the United States," CIA Director George Tenet framed the Colombian FARC threat in unusually stark terms:

  > Terrorism directed at U.S. interests goes beyond Middle Eastern or religious extremist groups. In our own hemisphere . . . the FARC has shown a new willingness to inflict casualties on U.S. nationals. . . . And the drug trade will continue to thrive until Bogotá can exert control over its vast countryside. FARC insurgents are well-financed by drugs and kidnappings, and they are increasingly using terrorism against civilians and economic targets . . . to wear away the new national will to fight back.[25]

- Some experts have even hinted that "the next battleground for U.S. forces could be in America's backyard—with South American drug-producing cartels the principle targets," and have speculated that "the war's objectives would include eliminating the threat the cartels' well-armed protectors pose to legitimate South American governments, and severing the drug-runners' links to organized international terrorist networks and organizations."[26]

In short, we can draw several common-sense conclusions from the example provided by Colombia. First, the narcotics-terrorism link is real; second, the link undermines stability in Colombia and across the region, perhaps even globally; third, the connection between drugs and terrorism in Colombia affects Americans by delivering narcotics to U.S. soil—where they claim thousands of lives annually—and by empowering terrorists who then target Americans.[27] Complicating matters even further, reports in June 2003 indicated that Colombia's AUC terrorist organization, widely described as an indigenous "counterinsurgency movement," is officially gaining "as much as 80 percent of [its] funding . . . from drug trafficking . . . [and that] the paramilitary movement is no longer principally an anti-insurgency force, but that most of its interests are focused on expanding its ties to the drug trade."[28]

MEXICO AND THE UNITED STATES: METHAMPHETAMINE, BLACK TAR HEROIN, MARIJUANA, AND TERRORISM

Like Colombia, Mexico shares an uneasy bond with the United States. Beyond geographic proximity and cultural similarities, both Colombia and Mexico lie at the heart of North America's narcotics epidemic. As a result, both countries suffer mightily the violence that attends narcotics distribution and abuse. By way of example, Mexico's secretary of public safety recently declared that drug trafficking "is destroying us [Mexico] as a nation and the main victims of this brutal business are children and young people."[29]

Specifically, Mexico is a major source of methamphetamine, black tar heroin, and marijuana consumed in the United States and Mexico. Mexico also serves as the major overland transshipment route for Colombian cocaine and heroin to the United States. Perhaps most significantly, Mexican criminal organizations smuggle vast quantities of "precursor chemicals"—the chemicals used to make synthetic drugs—into the United States. While marijuana is often "laced" with synthetic drugs and generates income for the same criminal organizations, synthetics are a major source of drug-trafficking income.

Synthetic drugs include methamphetamine, Ecstasy or MDMA, and GHB, as well as numerous other chemically synthesized narcotics. All can be deadly—and they are for thousands of young Americans each year.[30]

Among synthetic drugs, one of the most devastating to the human body and mind is methamphetamine (and its various subforms), often produced in clandestine "super-labs" in California and other states. The strongest tie between Mexico's violent drug-trafficking organizations—themselves terrorizing individuals and communities—and global terrorism is probably the money trail left by those trafficking in methamphetamine and precursor chemicals.

Perhaps the best evidence of Mexican and American pseudoephedrine and methamphetamine trafficking organizations financing global terrorism—in a major way—was the cracking of a California-based terrorism-financing ring in 2002. The investigation by California's Department of Justice produced riveting evidence of the link, and how the purchase of this drug in the United States fuels terrorist cells worldwide.

CALIFORNIA DRUG RING LINKED TO MIDDLE EAST

The California pseudoephedrine and methamphetamine case reinforced the Middle Eastern connection to U.S. drug profits. The nature of the connection was different from the indictments handed up in late 2002 against two Pakistanis and one American seeking stinger missiles for Al Qaeda in what was called a "missiles-for-drugs" exchange.

By contrast, the pseudoephedrine and methamphetamine investigation involved the use of drug money to support terrorism directly, through a series of money transfers to Middle Eastern terrorist groups.

In short, a different set of surprises emerged. According to the official report, "Narco-Terrorism in California: The Middle Eastern Connection," California is struggling with a more deeply rooted problem: "Yemeni, Jordanian and Palestinian pseudoephedrine [drug] traffickers are the primary [terrorist-related] groups operating in California."[31]

More specifically, a well-organized network was discovered trafficking these drugs from Canada to California, usually through Illinois and Michigan. This network produced drug revenue through "transnational cell structures" in California. The drug money generated was then "funneled to the Middle East through . . . a Middle Eastern inter-communal process that bypasses traditional government methods of recording and tracking the funds."[32]

So there can be no mistake about where the funds were headed, the report found: "Points of destination for these funds include Yemen, Israel, Brazil and Jordan—countries that have been infiltrated by terrorist organizations such as the Islamic Resistance Movement, also known as Hamas; Hezbollah; and al Qaeda."[33]

The California Justice Department report also reached conclusions about the nature of the link. Trends that investigators unearthed included these:

- "Middle Eastern pseudoephedrine trafficking organizations are composed of Middle Eastern males" of varying ages, including second-generation immigrants with knowledge of Spanish.
- "Primary countries of origin for members of pseudoephedrine trafficking organizations . . . were Yemen, Jordan and Israel (Palestinian). . . ."
- The trafficking organizations have "cell structures," keeping knowledge of "main leaders [and] financiers" from "drivers and distributors."
- "All financial transactions [and] money laundering activities are conducted exclusively through Middle Eastern networks."

- Certain pseudoephedrine traffickers accept "methamphetamine as a form of payment" and presumably resell the methamphetamine for profit.
- New York and Michigan serve as "major centers for laundering"—or hiding the source of—drug profits, "and these profits are sent to the Middle East."
- "Large amounts of U.S. currency are smuggled out of the United States through disguised containers, furniture, toys, and body carriers."[34]

Finally, although directly tying Middle Eastern terrorist groups to U.S. and Mexican drug traffickers was the biggest part of this investigation, the report also notes: "Middle Eastern terrorist organizations . . . have extensive operations in various geographic areas—including South America." In fact, confirming other law enforcement assessments, "the area bordering Paraguay, Argentina and Brazil—the tri-border area—has become a haven for groups such as Hizballah and HAMAS."[35]

No doubt, a great deal of what is actually known about drug trafficking and its ties to international terrorism remains hidden from the general public. Still, the evidence of a strong drug-terrorism connection in North and South America is increasingly clear. If further information were made public, ongoing investigations might be upset and plots to traffic and terrorize might not be stopped. That said, there is considerable evidence that the tie, as it relates to the United States, Mexico, Colombia, Bolivia, Peru, Paraguay, Argentina, Brazil, Canada, and other points in the Western Hemisphere, is real and troubling. Understanding the trend lines adds important context.

6

Identifying Trends in the Drugs-Terrorism Relationship

Although a number of potentially important trends have popped up in recent years, each one suggesting tighter bonds between drug traffickers and terrorists, several are worthy of special attention.

First, the "convergence" between terrorists and drug traffickers appears to be growing.[1] In other words, if the two groups have always overlapped slightly, they now seem to overlap substantially. If represented by circles drawn on a piece of paper, the overlap would have been nominal until recently, but now seems almost concentric at times. In fact, some experts wonder if terrorist organizations are not, in fact, simply developing drug-trafficking arms to fund their operations directly or, in some cases, becoming one and the same organization.

Second, key measures of drug purity are continuing to rise in many places across the globe, not least in the United States. With rising drug availability comes higher street purity, allowing drug traffickers and terrorist organizations to benefit from a growing, increasingly addicted, and retooled (now more lucrative) source of revenue.

Third, a new urgency surrounds the task of bringing antidrug and antiterrorism issues into international diplomacy, as well as into national security assessments. As

The author flying over coca fields in Colombia by helicopter on an official U.S. government trip. The Colombian government is seeking to eradicate coca. Colombian coca is processed into cocaine, then smuggled into the United States by drug traffickers. Money from cocaine and heroin sales in the United States returns to Colombia, where it is used to fund terrorism.

Huey II helicopters, of the kind used by U.S. and Colombian teams to eradicate coca plants and heroin poppies. The helicopters are armed to defend against FARC terrorists, who participate in and profit from drug production and trafficking activities in Colombia.

Rural Peru, and a rail line running toward Machu Picchu. In rural Peru, large quantities of coca are grown, then processed into coca paste and smuggled to Colombia for shipment by drug traffickers to the United States. The rail line seen here was often the object of attacks by Shining Path terrorists during the 1980s and early 1990s.

U.S. Drug Enforcement Administration officers work with Colombia's National Police to make Colombia more secure from the violence of drug traffickers.

A delegation of U.S. members of Congress watches as enormous quantities of coca paste are confiscated by DEA agents and local authorities in Bolivia during a 1997 visit. Pictured are Congressman Rod Blagoiavich (looking into the camera at foreground), who would later become governor of Illinois; Congressman Mark Souder (wearing white hat, glasses, and striped shirt), who would become chair of the U.S. House Drug Policy Subcommittee; Congressman J. Dennis Hastert (light hair, glasses, and jacket, beside Souder), who would become U.S. Speaker of the House; the author (beside Hastert, wearing a checkered shirt); two DEA agents stationed in Bolivia; and Rob Mobley, a leading U.S. Coast Guard officer working with Hastert (tall man in hat at rear).

Flying by helicopter over coca seedbeds in Colombia and Bolivia, South America.

In Bolivia, coca plants are often obscured by legitimate plant growth and tended by low-income rural growers. These growers receive only a small fraction of the profits made by drug traffickers, but often have insufficient infrastructure (such as roads, transportation, processing resources, and plantings) to support farming in legitimate cash crops.

The future U.S. Speaker of the House, Congressman J. Dennis Hastert, leads an oversight delegation to the Middle East in 1997. Here, he asks tough questions and examines firsthand the devastation caused by a terrorist bombing of U.S. quarters in Dhahran, Saudi Arabia.

At Camp Doha in Kuwait, in 1997, the author explored "force protection" and antiterrorism issues as part of a congressional oversight delegation led by now–U.S. Speaker of the House J. Dennis Hastert. The aim of this oversight effort was to examine counterterrorism and counterdrug policies in seven countries of the Middle East.

Aboard the U.S.S. *Nimitz* aircraft carrier in the Persian Gulf, the author and other members of the congressional oversight delegation exploring counterterrorism issues watch F-18s and F-14s launch to patrol the "Southern No-Fly Zone" over Iraq (1997).

Former President Ronald Reagan, who, with First Lady Nancy Reagan, led a decade of successful antidrug activity—on both supply reduction and education—shares a light moment with the author in Reagan's California office (1993).

Terrorism and the heroin sales that help fund it have long been linked in public dialogue. This 2001 cartoon, published at a time when "white powder" in boxes or envelopes connoted deadly anthrax, makes the point effectively.

national policies on everything from money laundering and crime prevention to environmental protection and immigration have been affected by drugs and terrorism, the need to keep these issues—and their nexus—front and center is growing. The lives of everyday Americans have increasingly been affected by the drug-terrorism link, as the drive for more money from drug sales has simultaneously increased health-care costs, insurance costs, crime costs, preventive and responsive costs to blunt drug trafficking and future terrorism.

CONVERGENCE OF DRUG TRAFFICKERS AND TERRORISTS

Consider what growing interaction between terrorists and drug traffickers—through Al Qaeda, Hezbollah, Hamas, the FARC, the ELN, and others in places like the Middle East, South America, and the United States—could mean.

Empirically, the threat of terrorism on our soil and to Americans abroad is reduced when we deprive terrorists of access to bank financing—by freezing their accounts and tracing official money flows. On the other hand, what if these groups become proficient at executing large, non-bank drug-trafficking operations and begin to piggyback terrorism financing on the drug-trafficking infrastructure that exists for heroin, cocaine, methamphetamine, and marijuana in the United States and Europe? What if the terrorist networks become more closely aligned with each other, and collectively aligned with narcotics trafficking organizations active in North America and Europe? Clearly, if the two sets of actors cooperated in more ways than they do now—for financial or ideological reasons—the implications could be grave. Examples to learn from are the negative effects of such a synergy in Colombia and Afghanistan.

Directly on point is a thoughtful analysis by terrorism expert Jessica Stern. In the July/August 2003 edition of *Foreign Affairs*, Stern points out the growing significance of South America as hub for future terrorist activities. Writing on the convergence of different terrorist elements, she notes:

> The triborder region of South America has become the world's new Libya, a place where terrorists with widely disparate ideologies—Marxist Colombian rebels, American white supremacists, Hamas, Hezbolah, and others—meet to swap tradecraft. . . . Moneys raised for terrorist organizations in the United States are often funneled through Latin America, which has also become an important stopover point for operatives entering the United States.[2]

While the phenomenon of convergence may only be in early development at this point, the longer-term implications are significant.

GREATER DRUG PURITY AND AVAILABILITY: MORE MONEY TO TERRORISTS

Street purities for Colombian and Mexican heroin, cocaine, and marijuana have been climbing markedly over the past two decades in the United States, and availability climbed dramatically during the 1990s. Similar effects can be seen now in Europe and Central Asia, resulting from higher heroin and opium production under the new Afghan regime.[3]

If national and international policies are not focused on recognizing the threat posed by such narcotics—reducing drug demand and prosecuting drug suppliers—then those who prey on unwitting users will have all the more to gain. Among this group will surely be the anti-Western and anti-American terrorist organizations.

Moreover, the less narcotics-consuming societies care about this issue, the more their indifference will affect other, neighboring societies. An obvious example in 2003 was the impact of European consumption on the societies of Central Asia. As *The Economist* reported, "with neighboring Afghanistan once again a major grower of opium, and demand for heroin still strong on the streets of Europe, Tajikistan and its neighbors are getting caught in the middle."[4] Similarly, indifference in any part of North America will affect both our South American neighbors and other parts of North America; conversely, indifference in South America or to the South American problem will affect the countries of North America.

The purity levels for these drugs has been maintained at a high level, even as availability has risen, chiefly because the policies of both consuming and producing countries have permitted the availability and purity to rise. The effect on contiguous and nearby societies is devastating. The ill-gotten income stream to those profiting is substantial. Thus, "Central Asia has become a major route for Afghan opium and heroin traveling to Europe," while "the value of heroin transiting has gone up by three to four times in 2002, reflecting an improvement in purity."[5] Not surprisingly, "since most local traffickers are paid in kind, the heroin trade leaves a trail of addicts in the transit countries of Central Asia."[6] Similar effects can be seen and felt across North, Central, and South America.

In a nutshell: Though not all drug traffickers are terrorists and not all funding for terrorism comes from narcotics, the higher the revenue from narcotics, the more attractive this source will be to terrorists and the more narcotics money will flow back to terrorist groups. Primary factors affecting revenue are availability, use and addiction rates in consumer societies, purity, and the costs imposed on producers and traffickers. Higher availability drives up use and addiction rates, increasing the demand for (and likelihood of) higher purity rates. Costs to traffickers rise with the increase in enforcement, interdiction, and prosecution, while revenue falls with sustained, successful prevention and the availability of comprehensive treatment regimes.

RECOGNIZING THE CENTRALITY OF NARCOTICS

In international diplomacy, as well as national security, terrorism and narcotics both deserve a central place. When leaders talk to the people they lead or to each other, these issues should be discussed. Since September 11, 2001, terrorism has been elevated to such a role, but narcotics and the narcotics-terrorism link have not.

In part, this reluctance to elevate narcotics and its link to terrorism is the result of foreign terrorism's sudden and shocking debut on American soil. In part, the reluctance to see narcotics as a substantial part of the threat matrix or overall picture may involve a bit of wishful thinking. Narcotics traffickers are hard to pin down, hard to stop entirely, somehow seem less ominous than bomb-wielding terrorists, and deliver a criminal product that some Americans and Europeans continue to consume.

But the importance of narcotics—including their link to organizations associated with terrorism, as well as their impact on individuals, families, communities, and nations—should not be downplayed. The prevalence of narcotics in a society serves as a warning indicator of that society's vulnerability to civic disorder, instability, and perhaps even a propensity for weakening moral resolve.

The cost of downplaying narcotics—measured by increased vulnerability to terrorism—is incalculable, but should be self-evident. Wider costs, such as those to emergency and long-term health care;[7] multiple levels of federal, state, and local law enforcement;[8] the environment;[9] and other societal "goods," such as character development[10] and labor productivity;[11] suggest that narcotics should be more central to conversations among leaders and citizens.[12] They especially belong in prevailing discussions of international diplomacy and national security. Too often, what has been missing is a comprehensive or global commitment to fighting terrorism and narcotics trafficking simultaneously. Any one nation or region confronting these threats needs the full cooperation of all nations in addressing them. If these threats are viewed in isolation, or as unconnected, they will both grow—to the detriment of the entire world.

7

Finding Solutions: What Won't Work

If narcotics and terrorism are so tightly linked—in so many dimensions, with documented cross-fertilization, and in so many locations—what can we do about it? What *should* we do about it—as a nation, as communities, and as individuals?

Finding real solutions, big and small ways to effectively deal with this link between terrorist organizations and drug traffickers, is important. Taking a bird's-eye view, we must ask: Are there policy options that serious-minded people would view as objectively reckless, ideas that should be shelved or dismissed for good reason?

At the same time, we must also ask: Are there obvious, available options that could realistically and objectively weaken the link between narcotics traffickers and terrorist organizations? Would such options improve our general security, safety, and health? Would they help us protect ourselves as a nation, as communities, as families, and as individuals?

UNLIKELY OPTIONS: THE NEED TO AVOID RECKLESSNESS

While it may seem obvious to some, the notion of standing by while narcotics traffickers and terrorists become more closely aligned is more than just reckless—it is certain to accelerate acts of terrorism and narcotics distribution. Neither outcome is one that Americans should want for themselves, their families, their communities, their nation, or the global community. Action is therefore the only real choice. But *what* action?

Before we get there, consider the other easy way out, one that seems to gain more glib adherents every day: Why not simply legalize narcotics—remove all the legal restrictions on production and sale, as well as the penalties—and, in the words of the eager few, "take the profit out of drug trafficking"?

COMMON SENSE AGAINST LEGALIZING NARCOTICS

Now *there* would be a neat trick—vanquishing an entire class of crimes by making them legal! If it would work for narcotics, then why not for robbery, burglary, rape, and homicide? More seriously, do we really want the government to be in the business of "trafficking" or administering dangerous and destructive drugs? For whom would such drugs be legal—just adults? Who would pay for the explosive increase in social costs associated with predictable increases in use? Who would cover the sudden spike in overdoses, emergency-room incidents, underweight births, infectious diseases, drug treatment programs, auto and workplace accidents, reduced labor productivity, lower educational achievement, crimes committed under the influence of drug use and addiction, elevated family dysfunction, increased domestic and child abuse—and human heartbreak?

Even more simply: Why wouldn't the legal drug market be subject to the same forces as every other legal market? How would legalization end the inevitable demand for purer and cheaper drugs—and more of them—than the government was willing to provide? Or the inevitable black market for narcotics below the government's "go-ahead-and-use" or "go-ahead-and-get-addicted" age? Or the obvious market for drugs so dangerous that even the government would not sanction their use? Or control over the various markets dominated by those outside the United States? In short, who would control the multilevel, still illegal, markets? The answer is the same people who control them today—drug traffickers and terrorist organizations—but with the difference that the American (and perhaps the European) markets would be *larger.* As more Americans tried these addictive substances, more would become addicted, a course extremely difficult to reverse once availability drives up use, elevating the aggregate number of people annually becoming addicted.

The end result would be a very sick nation, young and old, but one with enough wealth to keep buying until the combination of internal societal breakdown (economic and moral) and external threats, including terrorists flush with more drug money, brought the whole sad chapter to an end.

No—applying the principles of common sense, legalizing addictive drugs would not be prudent government. It would be reckless or, worse, an open invitation to national demise. We need not wander down that dark alley, since formal economics suggests answers elsewhere.

FORMAL ECONOMICS AGAINST LEGALIZING NARCOTICS

Okay, buckle up. Here we go. In formal economic terms, the central problem with drug legalization can be expressed as follows:

Every consumer of an addictive substance begins with a *first use* of that substance. That decision is informed by the costs of use, including price, risk of addiction and other perceived adverse health effects, and perceived benefits of use. As the consumer migrates from treating an addictive substance (for example, cocaine, heroin, or marijuana) as a "luxury" to treating that same substance as a "necessity," substantial research indicates that the "price elasticity of demand" (PED) for the drug shrinks—that is, price has less of an effect on the decision to use.

Unlike the first-time user of drugs, who is assumed to have weighed the addictive substance's putative effects against costs and risks, often based on information (accurate and inaccurate) collected from peers, media, parents, and the community at large, an addicted person's decision-making is circumscribed by his or her addiction. The addicted person's role as a purchaser or consumer is quickly *defined by* his or her addiction.

The laws of supply and demand, requiring rational economic or consumer behavior, do not work when applied to the addicted consumer, to whom price becomes less important. Consistent with the clinically proven elements of addiction, including dependence and tolerance, the market as applied to this consumer is no longer characterized by free and rational choice. The PED has fallen to a low point; large changes in price do not affect the addicted person's demand for the addictive substance or commodity.

Now, where does that leave the legalization option? In short, we can expect a few simple outcomes from policy choices that lead this way, whether they comprehend full legalization or merely a reduction in penalties. Policies that lower the price of addictive substances tend to increase first-time use, or initiation rates, for these substances. Increased use or initiation rates tend to increase addiction rates, based on the responsiveness of first-time and casual users to lower prices. All this assumes an unchanged quantity, but legalizing such substances (or lowering penalties for use and addiction) would increase availability, accelerating both use and addiction.

We can also say that, while raising prices of an addictive substance appears to lower the rate of first-time use or initiation for most addictive substances, higher prices do not appear to have any substantial impact on consumption by an already addicted population. Substitution of one addictive substance for another (similarly addictive) substance by an addicted population appears more likely at higher prices or in the event of lower availability. At the same time, "substitution" might include accessible, affordable treatment to end the addiction, when such an option is available; this is less likely to occur where significant effort is required by an addicted person to obtain treatment necessary to end the addiction.

In the end, rational or "free" choice by the addicted population appears to be significantly impaired by a combination of the cognitive deficit produced by using addictive substances (i.e., cognitive changes in brain function developing as a result of use of the addictive substance) and what is generally described as compulsion, a combination of dependence and growing tolerance to the addictive substance. Finally, there is this: Most discussants of legalization or government distribution of addictive substances do not take into account either (1) the predictable long-term growth in the population of addicted persons, or (2) the long-term addiction costs associated with the varying degrees of this policy choice.

In everyday terms, which economists seldom use, these ideas can be illustrated simply. The first rule is: Narcotics invariably slide down the so-called "price elasticity scale"—starting as a luxury and ending up a necessity. This rule may be illustrated by an analogy.

Marijuana, cocaine, and heroin are highly addictive substances,[1] whereas baseball games, carnival rides, and cotton candy are not. If prices rise on baseball tickets, carnival rides, or cotton candy—especially if the price rise is substantial—then buyers do not buy. Similarly, if prices are high for drugs, *first-time* purchasers act in the same way as nonaddicted buyers would act for any nonaddictive commodity, such as baseball, carnival tickets, or cotton candy: They do not buy.

On the other hand, regardless of increases in price, *addicted* persons exhibit far less freedom—if any—not to buy. Physiological and psychological dependencies dictate that higher prices will not deter buying or consuming. Data from both addictive science and criminal justice support this conclusion. Accordingly, drug-addicted persons do not choose *not* to buy drugs as prices rise, since that is typically no longer viewed as an option.

So, while lower prices may spur buying of drugs by non-addicted persons[2] and higher prices appear to reduce first-time buying among nonaddicts,[3] there is strong evidence that higher prices do not reduce buying by increasingly addicted persons. The implications of this argument are simply put: If narcotics of any kind were legalized, based on the addictive nature of these substances, several economic effects could be accurately predicted from low PEDs associated with these substances among addicted persons.

First, lower prices would drive a wider number of initial users to consume these substances.[4] Estimates by economists range upward from 8 percent of the population who, for purely economic reasons, would begin use at the lower prices created by legalization.[5]

Even those economic thinkers who advocate legalization of addictive substances seem to concede that prices would fall and availability would rise. *The Economist*, for example, conceded in July 2001 that legalizing narcotics "would increase the number of people who took them, whatever restrictions were applied," on top of raising "difficult questions about who should distribute them and how." Still, many advocates seem unmoved by the argument that initiation rates will increase. There seems little concern that the PED for any *one* of countless addictive narcotics would rapidly slide from high to low as addiction spread. Even *The Economist*, which has elsewhere advocated such an approach, accepts this fact:

> The number of drug users would rise for three reasons. First, the price of legalized drugs would almost certainly be lower—probably much lower—than the present price of illegal ones. . . . Second, access to legalized drugs would be easier. . . . And third, the social stigma against the use of drugs—which the law today helps to reinforce—would diminish. Many more people might try drugs if they did not fear imprisonment or scandal.[6]

Initially, this would amount to a new wave of freely made decisions, based on the information available from a variety of sources. The initial decision to use by these nonusers would weigh perceived costs and benefits, and produce, in some percentage of the population, a decision to begin use of the narcotic. Even conservative estimates of the percentage of first-time purchasers likely to become addicted, shows an enormous—some would say ominous—spike. The number of users and impact of legalization on addiction rates, objectively measurable social costs, and even such banal factors as state budgets, would be enormous. For these reasons, the narcotics legalization option is simply not an option—even in purely economic terms, it is a nonstarter.

8

Finding Solutions: What Might Work

PROMISING OPTIONS: NATIONWIDE EDUCATION, BETTER LAW ENFORCEMENT AND BORDER PROTECTION, STRONGER INTERNATIONAL COOPERATION, MORE AND BETTER TREATMENT

Luckily, there are more promising options. In fact, they are not particularly complicated, and again find themselves grounded in common sense. If the relationship between terrorist organizations and narcotics traffickers is to be eroded, four promising options should be pursued.

Understanding why and how to be vigilant helps you, your community, and the nation prevent terrorist acts. Likewise, understanding how narcotics sales feed terrorist coffers and aspirations can lead us to think twice, as a nation, about the choices we make in the years ahead. This understanding may even help the least caring among us to see how buying or using narcotics underwrites an evil that we condemn for ourselves, our communities, and the nation.

A nationwide effort to objectively explain how terrorists are empowered, in a fairly concrete way, by *our* actions would be sobering. This kind of education takes time. It is especially difficult as America fights its way out of lingering uncertainty after the events of September 11, 2001. Already, there is enough information to make the point as it relates to drugs and terrorism: Such a tie, even if not yet fully defined, affects our national and personal security. As we approach a wide range of choices everyday, we should consider acting on that vital information. Knowledge is power, as Sir Francis Bacon told us[1]—but only if we act on it.

Whether acting on drug prevention information provided by experts like the Partnership for a Drug-Free America or security advisories of the new Department on Homeland Security, DEA, or State Department, there is an enduring value for each of us in staying well-informed. Smart choices and prescient actions depend, in the end, on the quality of the information upon which we rely. They also depend on our commitment, to others and ourselves, to make that information count.

Second, we should reinforce what we already *know* works. We, and most Europeans, know that many of the drugs in our respective countries—the same drugs funding terrorism in the Middle East and South America—do not come from the United States or Europe. In fact, even synthetics produced in the United States often require precursor chemicals from outside our country.

So we know another fact: If we can do a better job of securing our borders, especially here in the United States, we can turn back the biggest wave of support for drug traffickers and drug-funded terrorist groups. To do that, we must act—both as individuals and as a nation—to support our local, state, and federal law enforcement communities. In the end, what we do to help those in law enforcement do their jobs better will be returned manifold.[2]

Today, law enforcement is under tremendous pressure both because of the threat presented by terrorism, and because of the threat posed by those who traffic in narcotics. Narcotics officers—those who try to break the bond between drugs and terrorism, to track and prosecute the chain of distribution leading back to traffickers and terrorists—typically have fewer resources, more assignments, greater daily danger in their lives, and not much back-up. If ever they needed help, it would be at this time. Today, their jobs are among the most dangerous in the world, yet ironically are among the least recognized and rewarded.[3]

Since 2001, the FBI has redirected hundreds of its agents from domestic narcotics trafficking to more immediate terrorist targets.[4] The FBI, the Department of Homeland Security, the rest of the intelligence community, and even the Drug Enforcement Administration all must do this from time to time. As a result, a heavy burden now falls on those who track the movement of drug money to terrorists at home and abroad, such as state and local law enforcement agents, the Drug Enforcement Administration, the Financial Crimes Enforcement Network, U.S. Customs Service, and U.S. State Department's Office of International Narcotics and Law Enforcement.

Today, the federal government is leaning more and more heavily on state and local law enforcement officers—especially those who have information, experience, and local connections of value to the federal government—to help them collect, analyze, share, and make best use of current information. Together, many law enforcement officers are being tasked to use what they know about drug trafficking, money laundering, and terrorism to predict the next terrorist event.

Often underappreciated in this task—particularly while the nation seeks to return humanity and stability to Iraq—are the nation's unsung, but exceptional, narcotics officers. More specifically, as we push to sever the link between narcotics funding and terrorists, from the Middle East to South America, we should pause to see the parallel between U.S. military troops abroad and narcotics officers at home, both of whom risk their lives daily. Striking parallels may better illustrate the contribution that law enforcement makes in this unending battle.

For understandable reasons, we often forget that without narcotics officers on our streets and in our communities, there would be—in a word—anarchy. Too often, we forget the very real and timely parallels to our larger national security struggle.

Our nation's intense fight for the liberation of Iraq in 2003 offers a meaningful parallel to the battle joined by narcotics officers on the front lines of our own continent every day. Consider the similarities:

- In Iraq, our troops faced guerrilla warfare, as well as enemies who terrorized parents, targeted innocent children, disguised themselves in civilian clothes, carried the latest firearms, and had no respect for human life. Narcotics officers face these same realities—every day—when they confront drug traffickers.
- In Iraq, coalition soldiers confronted a foe capable of using weapons of mass destruction to kill thousands of innocent people to devastate and instill fear. Narcotics officers face a similar foe when dealing with distributors of methamphetamine, heroin, crack cocaine, Ecstasy, and the like.
- Coalition soldiers in Iraq faced psychological warfare—or "psyops"—by an adversary seeking to deceive, confuse, and weaken the civilian population's resolve in confronting acts of inhumanity and injustice. Coalition troops faced an adversary that tried desperately to obscure clear-headedness and win by deception. Narcotics officers face the same sort of foe when they confront those who wish to obscure the links between drugs and terrorism, or minimize the destruction caused by narcotics.
- In Iraq, coalition troops faced an adversary motivated by some of the basest human instincts, a regime that thought only of itself, and not about the rippling circles of lives lost or pain to survivors. Narcotics officers face a similar foe, as they confront the human carnage and pain created by drug traffickers, distributors, and dealers who directly profit from human suffering and encourage others to do the same.

- The adversary in Iraq willingly drove its own country and communities into financial ruin, exploding oil wells, buildings, and infrastructure; gassing dissidents; and spreading the costs of rampant crime. The regime was indifferent to the severity of economic damage done to those it dared to call countrymen. Similarly, narcotics traffickers and those who aid and abet them collectively weigh down the nation's health-care system, emergency rooms, treatment facilities, and state and federal law enforcement budgets through damage to people and property.

- The Iraqi regime vicitimized the innocent, stripping them of both their innocence and their freedom. Those who participate in the narcotics trade do the same. They promote addiction to the unsuspecting and unaware, creating victims who stand to lose both their innocence and the capacity to make informed decisions. Drug addicts give up their freedom of choice and free will for the tyranny of dependence and the sordid human behaviors that trail addiction.

- Like Hussein's regime in Iraq, narcotics traffickers are indifferent to the American system of values, including protection of freedom, the environment, and the safety of children in everyday settings. Methamphetamine "super-labs" pollute mountain ranges in states like California and Oregon; methamphetamine cookers endanger young lives with volatile, often explosive, precursors; Colombian cocaine producers maintain thousands of maceration pits,[5] polluting tens of thousands of square miles of South America's pristine rivers and rain forests; and countless lives have been lost.

- Both the former Iraqi regime and narcotics trade ignore the human rights of women—subjugating, using, and disrespecting them on a daily basis. The narcotics trade contributes heavily to the 80 percent of domestic violence tied to substance abuse, and reduces the status of women in other ways, denying them the decency that civilized societies accord all humanity.
- In Iraq, coalition troops faced an adversary that killed thousands of its own people. Narcotics officers face a similar adversary—20,000 young lives were lost last year to drug abuse and drug-related crime, not including those killed in the line of duty by drug traffickers in Colombia, Mexico, the United States, and elsewhere.
- Finally, our troops in Iraq took risks for others based on positive motivations—not for victory parades or some outpouring of national gratitude, but because it was *the right thing to do.* To paraphrase a thought attributed to the Irish-British statesman Edmund Burke, the only thing it takes for evil to prevail is for good people to do nothing. The same motivations generally inspire those who take risks for others as domestic law enforcement officers.

The central point is this: Securing a nation against attacks from abroad and from within requires a similar commitment, sacrifice, and level of knowledge—and should engender similar public appreciation. In fact, few Americans realize what the world would be like without law enforcement officers daily protecting them. Moreover, progress against grave threats to our national security is usually incremental, not sudden. This is true of all struggles against evil—from narcotics-funded terrorism to simple acts of human violence. Generally, we do not win once and for all, living happily ever after in a world where threats, such as those posed by narcotics or terrorism, have been permanently vanquished. Rather, we go home, aware that we must remain at the ready, safe for today, until hard choices are again presented tomorrow.

Our reward, and that of law enforcement officers, is in knowing that the battle has been joined, that we are vigilant and armed against a real and dangerous adversary, that our own good choices can stand between that which is destructive and those we love. Historically, Americans owe a great deal to those who protect our national security, in places like Iraq and Afghanistan. In a like way, we owe our law enforcement community—narcotics officers in particular—a debt of honor and support.

But, how can *we* act on this analogy? How can ordinary citizens assist and reinforce the values and actions of those who work daily to break the threat matrix presented by narcotics funding and terrorists? One way, as indicated above, is vigilance. Another is responsible individual decision-making—if the action you would take adds to the net weight of their burden, don't take it. If it would help them, or have no effect, go ahead. Third, consider the power of being well-informed. Rely on sound and well-documented information when making decisions large and small, from what you will do with your day to what you may contribute to national security. As in other matters, those who have solid information hold the upper hand.

In a broader sense, we all need to do what we can, despite the stresses of the moment, to think more about how to handle this mammoth problem in an effective and consistent way.

International cooperation may not be in fashion, and it may seem awfully distant from where you sit now, but it matters. Individually, we may not sit at the United Nations, work at the State Department, speak a foreign language, serve in Congress or a state legislature, or be able to tell the president of the United States (or any other country) just how much we think this issue matters; but we *can* talk about it with peers, parents, teachers, community leaders, and maybe even our congressional representatives. We can say, "Hey, this issue matters to us, as Americans." In the end, we can tackle some problems as individuals, more as families and communities, and still a larger number as a nation. This is one issue that will call out the best from all civilized members of the international community, if we are to sever the relationship between violent drug traffickers and ruthless terrorist organizations.

Finally, better drug treatment options for those Americans who have been caught in the spiderweb of addiction, there to languish without help, are needed. Though there is insufficient room here to discuss this vital topic in the detail it deserves, consider simply Ralph Waldo Emerson's observation that "every man is an empire." No one should be left behind in our national effort to stop the destructive forces of drug addiction and terrorism. Those caught in the web of addiction must be freed, even as we collectively fight to free and protect our nation. In practical terms, this means that we must see the pain of addiction as it is. Addiction affects individuals, families, communities, and the nation. We must be proactive in reaching out to those who suffer, consciously bringing along members of society who need our help, if we are to make the society itself healthier, safer, and more predictably secure.

9

Closing Ideas

A few closing ideas are worthy of special mention. Although they cannot be fully explored here, they deserve a robust discussion. They closely shadow the solutions, as well as the threats, described in the previous chapters.

HOW FAR SHOULD GOVERNMENTS GO TO BREAK THE LINK BETWEEN DRUG TRAFFICKERS AND TERRORISTS? ARE THERE LIMITS?

We could rightly read and speak all day about the importance of civil and human rights. As a nation and as individuals, we understand and believe in them. Respect for the Bill of Rights and the values embodied in the U.S. Constitution is fundamental to our society's survival. Of course, we could spend equal time exploring how civil and human rights have evolved over the centuries, ebbing and flowing in response to domestic crises and wartime pressures, even across the history of the United States.

If terrorism on our soil has put us in a state of continuing—perhaps indefinite—war with those who would kill or harm us, the task of balancing fundamental rights against survival and protection stands as a continuing challenge. Far from a reduced effort, that challenge calls for more effort from each of us.

SEVERAL IDEAS TO KEEP IN MIND

First, the texts of the U.S. Constitution and the Bill of Rights, including guarantees offered to individuals in those precious documents, do not change. Human interpretation may cause these documents to bend and wobble at times, especially in the chilly breeze of war, but core values should not be viewed as relative, shifting, or changeable. They are not. Those pivotal "truths" are still "self-evident," and those precious rights are still immutable. Working to give the government and one another patience and latitude, at this and in future stressful times, is an enduring challenge.

Second, respect for human rights is a value Americans hold dear, beyond the text of the Constitution. Historically, a special regard for human rights exists outside of legal imperatives, and even when there are pressures to cast them aside. In times of war, the United States has always struggled to spare civilians; to balance the rights of those conquered against the nation's physical security; and to fairly mete out justice, even if that requires super-human patience. We are in such a place now.

That respect, of course, cannot obscure our collective right to self-defense or the defense of others, but it is fair to say that new moral questions never previously in front of us will continue to appear. Moral choices, human rights, self-defense, and the proper defense of others will each, at different times, weigh on our minds—nowhere more than in the battle to beat drug traffickers and terrorists. As a general matter, the complexity of life should not cause us, as a nation or as individuals, to retreat into the snare of easy, but wrong-headed, answers. We must continue to do the hard thinking, hard balancing, and hard decision-making that difficult times demand. In this effort, there will continue to be a high premium on getting facts right and talking to each other from common facts.

Third, no act by our government or by a terrorist can ever relieve us of the individual responsibility to do the right thing. Whether that requirement is in the context of defending the nation or defending an ideal in casual conversation, whether that reality triggers the need to write your congressional representative, start a community coalition, assist a friend, or steer clear of some action, the point remains the same. Whether in time of war or peace, at home, school, work, or recreation, the obligation of citizens to exercise individual responsibility for their own actions and to assist others in the society is paramount. In a time of national stress, the obligation is still higher.

Central to the link between narcotics and terrorism is one last, nagging fact: As a nation, we must be willing to project ourselves around the globe diplomatically and militarily, but also to pry ourselves from the sources of terrorist funding we have grown accustomed to overlooking. Only by seeing this link, understanding its significance, and taking a stand against it can we hope to free ourselves from two of the greatest threats this nation has ever faced: narcotics and terrorism. You now know the incontrovertible links, the logic behind the links, and the urgency of the national need to move forward with eyes open, acting on the best information available, to make wise decisions on a treacherous sea.

Together, narcotics traffickers and terrorists present a formidable adversary. Nevertheless, Americans can defeat them both and restore security, health, and safety to our homes, communities, and the nation. Terrorists, funded by drug money, represent a predator much like a shark. The lethality of the jaws depends directly on the support of the dorsal fin. Absent the dorsal fin, the shark flounders. We can end the parallel connection between terrorism and drugs by acknowledging the connection's existence, refusing to accept it, and acting to separate the jaws from fin. In such a world, we will all swim more safely.

CHAPTER 2: WHO ARE TERRORISTS?

1 See 22 *United States Code,* Section 2656f(d)(2).

2 "I shall not today attempt further to define the kinds of material I understand to be embraced within [a certain category of pornography]; and perhaps I could never succeed in intelligibly doing so. But I know it when I see it. . . ." *Jacobellis* v. *Ohio,* 378 U.S. 184 (1964) (Stewart, J., concurring).

3 Partnership for a Drug-Free America, *Partnership Bulletin* (November 2001):1 (statistics drawn from a nationally projectable telephone survey of 800 parents and 500 teens age 12 to 17). Notably, such research affirms the value of television advertising on this topic. By way of example, one strategist for the Partnership for a Drug-Free America noted that such numbers are "significant [because] greater exposure to the facts may have a positive impact on two of the nation's top concerns, drugs and terrorism," adding that such numbers show "teen respondents were highly conscientious" when they knew the facts. Interview with Benjamin Bawden, advisor to the Partnership for a Drug-Free America.

4 This list can be accessed online via the Department of State at *www.state.gov/s/ct/rls/fs/2003/17067.htm.*

5 "Law Enforcement Guide to Terrorist Groups and Their Known Emblems," *NESPIN Law Enforcement Bulletin* 8:6(November/December 2002), citing Paul Jordan, Texas Department of Public Safety, Special Crimes Service, Austin, Texas.

6 See *The Los Angeles Times,* June 10, 2003, "Al Qaeda Attack Highly Probable, U.S. Says." Moreover, one leading expert noted in the July/August edition of *Foreign Affairs,* the premier publication of the Council on Foreign Relations, that "al Qaeda and its affiliates remain among the most significant threats to U.S. national security today." The expert notes of Al Qaeda: "Perhaps most surprising (and alarming) is the increasing evidence that al Qaeda, a Sunni organization, is now cooperating with the Shi'a group Hezbollah, considered to be the most sophisticated terrorist group in the world," adding that "Hezbollah . . . enjoys backing from Syria and Iran, is based in southern Lebanon and in the lawless 'triborder' region of South America, where Paraguay, Brazil, and Argentina meet . . . [and] has also maintained a fundraising presence in the United States since the 1980s." Jessica Stern, "The Protean Enemy," *Foreign Affairs,* July/August 2003, p. 27.

7 "Law Enforcement Guide to Terrorist Groups and Their Known Emblems," *NESPIN Law Enforcement Bulletin* 8:6 (November/December 2002).

8 "Traffickers Turn From Balkan Conduit to 'Northern' Route," *Jane's Intelligence Review* (August 2001): 27.

9 Ibid.

10 With substantial stockpiles to rely on, the Taliban cut production in 2001, before the government's demise. "That prohibition, which came after several years in which the Taliban quietly encouraged poppy farming, cut opium from an estimated 4,042 tons in 2000, about 71 percent of the world's supply, to just 82 tons [in 2001]. . . ." ("U.S. Fears Afghan Farmers Can't End Cash Crop: Opium," *The New York Times* [April 1, 2002]) However, experts noted that this was more likely an effort to control the price of heroin on the world market than a lasting decline in availability. For example, Congressman Mark Souder (R-IN), chairman of the U.S. House Subcommittee on Drug Policy, noted that the Taliban's cut in production "appears in reality to be a coldly calculated ploy to control the market price for their opium and heroin." (Congressman Mark Souder, cited in "U.S.: Taliban Continues to Profit from Drug Trade," *CNN.com* [October 3, 2001]).

11 "Traffickers Turn From Balkan Conduit to 'Northern' Route," *Jane's Intelligence Review* (August 2001): 28.

12 Ibid.

13 Ibid.

14 Ibid., p. 29.

15 Asa Hutchinson, administrator, Drug Enforcement Administration, speech given at Arlington, Virginia (February 1, 2002).

16 Associated Press (AP) News, "As Disruption from War on Taliban Ends, Traffickers Moving Big Heroin Shipments" (January 14, 2002).

17 Associated Press (AP) News, "Afghans Harvest Bumper Crop of Opium" (March 8, 2002).

18 "Law Enforcement Guide to Terrorist Groups and Their Known Emblems," *NESPIN Law Enforcement Bulletin* 8:6 (November/December 2002), citing Paul Jordan, Texas Department of Public Safety, Special Crimes Service, Austin, Texas.

19 Steven Emerson, "Foreign Terrorists in America: Five Years After the World Trade Center Bombing," Testimony before the U.S. Senate Subcommittee on Terrorism, Technology, and Government Information (February 24, 1998); *see also* Steven Emerson, "An Investigation into the Operations of Terrorist Networks in the United States and Canada," Testimony before the U.S. House of Representatives Judiciary Subcommittee on Immigration and Claims (January 26, 2000).

20 "Five Detained in Philippine Bombing," *The Washington Post* (March 6, 2003): A12.

21 Steven Emerson, "Foreign Terrorists in America: Five Years After the World Trade Center Bombing," Testimony before the U.S. Senate Subcommittee on Terrorism, Technology, and Government Information (February 24, 1998).

22 Ibid.

23 See *Transcript of CNN.Com,* June 11, 2003, "Hamas Bombing, Israel Strikes Test Peace Efforts."

24 "Suicide Bomber Kills Fifteen on Bus in Northern Israel," *The Washington Post* (March 6, 2003): A12.

25 Ibid.

26 See "The Enemy Next Door," *Armed Forces Journal International* (March 2000): 40, p. 44, noting that "[b]ecause narco-traffickers and terrorist organizations often work hand-in-hand, their span of influence is truly international. Together, they have become the most powerful force in the criminal world." Adding to this sentiment is one observer's recent assessment that the individual, "Imad Mughniyah, who directs Hezbollah in the [South American] triborder area [of Paraguay, Brazil and Argentina], has also been appointed by Iran to coordinate the group's activities with Hamas and Palestinian Islamic Jihad." Jessica Stern, "The Protean Enemy," *Foreign Affairs,* July/August 2003, p. 32.

27 "Law Enforcement Guide to Terrorist Groups and Their Known Emblems," *NESPIN Law Enforcement Bulletin* 8:6 (November/December 2002), citing Paul Jordan, Texas Department of Public Safety, Special Crimes Service, Austin, Texas.

28 For example, one authoritative account notes that "drug money flowing to and from the Middle East and Eastern Europe is now believed to fund organizations ranging from Hizzballah affiliates to the Kosovo Liberation Army (KLA)." See "The Enemy Next Door," *Armed Forces Journal International* (March 2000): 40, p. 44.

29 Steven Emerson, "Foreign Terrorists in America: Five Years After the World Trade Center Bombing," Testimony before the U.S. Senate Subcommittee on Terrorism, Technology, and Government Information (February 24, 1998).

30 "Terrorism in Latin America," *The Star-Banner* (Ocala, Florida) (February 15, 2002).

31 "Narco-Terrorism in California: The Middle Eastern Connection," Group Analysis Report, California Department of Justice, Division of Law Enforcement, Criminal Intelligence Bureau (September 2002): 12.

32 *Testimony of Steven W. Casteel, Assistant Administrator for Intelligence, Before the Senate Committee on the Judiciary,* U.S. Congress, May 20, 2003, "Narco-Terrorism: International Drug Trafficking and Terrorism—A Dangerous Mix."

33 "Narco-Terror: The Worldwide Connection Between Drugs and Terror," *Joint Testimony of Assistant Secretary of State for International Narcotics and Law Enforcement, Rand Beers, and Ambassador-at-Large for Counterterrorism, Francis Taylor, before the Senate Committee on the Judiciary, Subcommittee on Technology, Terrorism and Government Information,* March 13, 2002.

34 "Hezbollah: 'A-Team of Terrorists', *Transcript of 60 Minutes,* April 18, 2003.

35 Ibid.

36 "Law Enforcement Guide to Terrorist Groups and Their Known Emblems," *NESPIN Law Enforcement Bulletin* 8:6 (November/December 2002), citing Paul Jordan, Texas Department of Public Safety, Special Crimes Service, Austin, Texas.

37 See "The Enemy Next Door," *Armed Forces Journal International* (March 2000): 40, p. 42.

38 "Law Enforcement Guide to Terrorist Groups and Their Known Emblems," *NESPIN Law Enforcement Bulletin* 8:6 (November/December 2002), citing Paul Jordan, Texas Department of Public Safety, Special Crimes Service, Austin, Texas.

39 *Testimony of Steven W. Casteel, Assistant Administrator for Intelligence, Before the Senate Committee on the Judiciary,* U.S. Congress, May 20, 2003, "Narco-Terrorism: International Drug Trafficking and Terrorism—A Dangerous Mix."

40 For example, the State Department concluded in 2002 that "there are strong indications that the FARC has established links with the Irish Republican Army to increase its capability to conduct urban terrorism." *See* "Narco-Terror: The Worldwide Connection Between Drugs and Terror," *Joint Testimony of Assistant Secretary of State for International Narcotics and Law Enforcement, Rand Beers, and Ambassador-at-Large for Counterterrorism, Francis Taylor, before the Senate Committee on the Judiciary, Subcommittee on Technology, Terrorism and Government Information,* March 13, 2002.

41 *Testimony of Steven W. Casteel, Assistant Administrator for Intelligence, Before the Senate Committee on the Judiciary,* U.S. Congress, May 20, 2003, "Narco-Terrorism: International Drug Trafficking and Terrorism—A Dangerous Mix."

42 "Law Enforcement Guide to Terrorist Groups and Their Known Emblems," *NESPIN Law Enforcement Bulletin* 8:6 (November/December 2002), citing Paul Jordan, Texas Department of Public Safety, Special Crimes Service, Austin, Texas.

43 Ibid.

44 The International Narcotics Control Strategy, or INCS, Bureau of International Narcotics and Law Enforcement, State Department, 1998; *see also* "Political Violence and Narco-Trafficking," Booklet, Paris Institute of Criminology, October, 1996; United Nations International Narcotics Control Board, or INCB, 1992 Report, paragraph 5 ("... illicit cultivation of narcotic plants and illicit trafficking in drugs continue to be a threat to the political, economic and social stability of several countries. ..."); "Narco-Terror: The Worldwide Connection Between Drugs and Terror," Joint Testimony of Assistant Secretary of State for International Narcotics and Law Enforcement, Rand Beers, and Ambassador-at-Large for Counterterrorism, Francis Taylor, before the Senate Committee on the Judiciary, Subcommittee on Technology, Terrorism and Government Information, March 13, 2002 ("The PKK 'taxes' ethnic Kurdish drug traffickers and individual cells traffic heroin to support their operations").

45 *Testimony of Steven W. Casteel, Assistant Administrator for Intelligence, Before the Senate Committee on the Judiciary,* U.S. Congress, May 20, 2003, "Narco-Terrorism: International Drug Trafficking and Terrorism—A Dangerous Mix."

46 For example, an unclassified Report of Audit by the Office of Inspector General at the Department of State found in December 1996 that—just when Peru's Shining Path terrorists were declining in influence—"Peru had significant success in interdicting the aerial flow of narcotics from Peru to Colombia ... resulting in significant price drops for coca base in country [Peru] and anecdotal evidence of widespread abandonment of coca fields. As coca production has increased again in recent years, there has been a rise also in terrorist activities in Peru." (Report of Audit [unclassified], "Review of the Counternarcotics Certification Process," Office of Inspector General, United States State Department, 7–CI–004, December 1996; *see Hearing before the Committee on International Relations of House of Representatives, 105th Congress, 2nd Session,* "U.S. Annual Drug Certification," April 29, 1998; "Illicit Drug Availability: Are Interdiction Efforts Hampered by a Lack of Agency Resources?," *Hearings before the Subcommittee on National Security, International Affairs, and Criminal Justice of the Committee on Government Reform and Oversight, House of Representatives, 104th Congress, 1st Session,* June 27–28, 1995.)

47 Ibid.

48 U.S. Department of State, Press Release, "State Department Officials Point to Drugs-Terrorism Ties in the Americas," March 13, 2002; *see also* "Narco-Terror: The Worldwide Connection Between

Drugs and Terror," *Joint Testimony of Assistant Secretary of State for International Narcotics and Law Enforcement, Rand Beers, and Ambassador-at-Large for Counterterrorism, Francis Taylor, before the Senate Committee on the Judiciary, Subcommittee on Technology, Terrorism and Government Information*, March 13, 2002.

49 "Law Enforcement Guide to Terrorist Groups and Their Known Emblems," *NESPIN Law Enforcement Bulletin* 8:6 (November/December 2002), citing Paul Jordan, Texas Department of Public Safety, Special Crimes Service, Austin, Texas.

50 "The New Threat of Organized Crime and Terrorism," *Jane's Terrorism & Security Monitor* (June 19, 2000).

51 Steven Emerson, "Foreign Terrorists in America: Five Years After the World Trade Center Bombing," Testimony before the U.S. Senate Subcommittee on Terrorism, Technology, and Government Information (February 24, 1998).

52 State Department officials have testified that "[t]he LTTE reportedly has close ties to drug trafficking networks in Burma, and Tamil expatriates may carry drugs in exchange for training from Burma, Pakistan and Afghanistan." *See* "Narco-Terror: The Worldwide Connection Between Drugs and Terror," *Joint Testimony of Assistant Secretary of State for International Narcotics and Law Enforcement, Rand Beers, and Ambassador-at-Large for Counterterrorism, Francis Taylor, before the Senate Committee on the Judiciary, Subcommittee on Technology, Terrorism and Government Information*, March 13, 2002.

53 According to 2002 State Department testimony, "The AUC umbrella group, which includes many Colombian paramilitary forces, admittedly uses the cocaine trade to finance its counterinsurgency campaign ... [and] AUC elements appear to be directly involved in processing cocaine and exporting cocaine from Colombia." *See* "Narco-Terror: The Worldwide Connection Between Drugs and Terror," *Joint Testimony of Assistant Secretary of State for International Narcotics and Law Enforcement, Rand Beers, and Ambassador-at-Large for Counterterrorism, Francis Taylor, before the Senate Committee on the Judiciary, Subcommittee on Technology, Terrorism and Government Information*, March 13, 2002. Moreover, recent reports indicate that the Colombian government itself has also reached this conclusion. A closely held report, made public in June 2003 by *The Washington Post*, indicates that "as much as 80 percent of the AUC's funding comes from drug trafficking," and that this group's origins and evolution are becoming more clear: "The AUC was a confederation of regional paramilitary groups that emerged across Colombia in response to the Marxist insurgency with a combined force of about 15,000 combatants. . . . Many paramilitary fighters once served in Colombia's military, including some of its top commanders ... [and] the [Colombian government] analysis says the paramilitary movement is no longer principally an anti-insurgency force, but that most of its interests are focused on expanding its ties to the drug trade." "Colombian Report Details Drug Trafficking by Paramilitary Forces," *The Washington Post*, June 26, 2003, p. A24.

54 "The New Threat of Organized Crime and Terrorism," *Jane's Terrorism & Security Monitor* (June 19, 2000).

55 "Narco-Terror: The Worldwide Connection Between Drugs and Terror," *Joint Testimony of Assistant Secretary of State for International Narcotics and Law Enforcement, Rand Beers, and Ambassador-at-Large for Counterterrorism, Francis Taylor, before the Senate Committee on the Judiciary, Subcommittee on Technology, Terrorism and Government Information*, March 13, 2002.

56 "Narco-Terror: The Worldwide Connection Between Drugs and Terror," *Joint Testimony of Assistant Secretary of State for International Narcotics and Law Enforcement, Rand Beers, and Ambassador-at-Large for Counterterrorism, Francis Taylor, before the Senate Committee on the Judiciary, Subcommittee on Technology, Terrorism and Government Information*, March 13, 2002.

57 *Testimony of Steven W. Casteel, Assistant Administrator for Intelligence, Before the Senate Committee on the Judiciary,* U.S. Congress, May 20, 2003, "Narco-Terrorism: International Drug Trafficking and Terrorism—A Dangerous Mix."

58 Steven Emerson, "Foreign Terrorists in America: Five Years After the World Trade Center Bombing," Testimony before the U.S. Senate Subcommittee on Terrorism, Technology, and Government Information (February 24, 1998); *see also* Steven Emerson, "An Investigation into the Operations of Terrorist Networks in the United States and Canada," Testimony before the U.S. House of Representatives Judiciary Subcommittee on Immigration and Claims (January 26, 2000).

59 "The New Threat of Organized Crime and Terrorism," *Jane's Terrorism & Security Monitor* (June 19, 2000).

60 See *Testimony of Steven W. Casteel, Assistant Administrator for Intelligence, Before the Senate Committee on the Judiciary,* U.S. Congress, May 20, 2003, "Narco-Terrorism: International Drug Trafficking and Terrorism—A Dangerous Mix."

CHAPTER 3: THE AMERICAN ADDICTION

1 "Teen Drug Use Declined in 2002, Report Shows," *NIDA Notes,* January 2003, Vol. 17, No. 5, p. 12.

2 "25 Arrested in Big Colombian Heroin Ring, Authorities Say," *The New York Times,* June 13, 2002, p. A32.

3 *National Household Survey on Drug Abuse,* HHS, 1997.

4 Drug Enforcement Administration, *National Narcotics Intelligence Consumers Committee Report (NNICC) 1997,* DEA-98036 (November 1998), pp. 39–40; *see also* Substance Abuse and Mental Health Services Administration (Rockville, MD), *Preliminary Estimates from the Drug Abuse Warning Network: 1995 Preliminary Estimates of Drug-Related Emergency Department Episodes* (1996).

5 The number and causes of death from illegal drug use are varied, including drug psychoses, drug dependence, nondependent drug abuse, neonatal drug withdrawal, accidental drug poisoning and overdose, other adverse drug effects, and accidental or purposeful injury or poisoning. *See* "Economic Costs of Drug Abuse," Rice, D.P., Kelman, S., & Miller, L.S. (1991), in Cartwright, W.S., & J.M. Kaple, eds., *Economic Costs, Cost-Effectiveness, Financing and Community-Based Drug Treatment,* NIDA Research Monograph No. 113 (Rockville, MD: U.S. Department of Health and Human Services). For overall costs and effects of various drugs, and the costs and effectiveness of treatment regimes. *See* "Socioeconomic Evaluations of Addictions Treatment, *The White House President's Commission on Model State Drug Laws,* December 1993 (available through the National Alliance for Model State Drug Laws, Alexandria, VA). Note that, by the late 1980s, the impact of drug abuse was considerable in purely economic terms. "For instance, Harwood (1991) found that cost-of-illness estimates for drug abuse in the United States rose from around $10 billion in studies published between 1973 and 1975, to $16.4 billion in 1977, to $46.9 billion in 1980, to $58.3 billion in 1988. This was nearly a six-fold increase that was not justified by any inflationary or epidemiological trend." "Socioeconomic Evaluations of Addictions Treatment, *The White House President's Commission on Model State Drug Laws,* December 1993, citing Harwood, H.J. (1991), "Economics and Drugs: Promises, Problems and Prospects," in Cartwright, W.S. & J.M. Kaple, (1991), *Economic Costs, Cost-Effectiveness, Financing and Community-Based Drug Treatment,* NIDA Research Monograph No. 113 (Rockville, MD: U.S. Department of Health and Human Services). By 1998, direct costs were put at $67 billion by the U.S. General Accounting Office. See *GAO Report: "Drug Abuse—Research Shows Treatment is Effective, but Benefits May Be Overstated,"* GAO/HEHS-98-72, March 1998, p. 1.

6 "Cocaine Use and Cardiovascular Complications," *Medical Journal of Australia,* Clinical Update (September 2, 2002); *see also* Substance Abuse and Mental Health Services Administration (Rockville, MD), *Preliminary Estimates from the Drug Abuse Warning Network: 1995 Preliminary Estimates of Drug-Related Emergency Department Episodes* (1996).

7 See *Marihuana And Medicine,* ed. Gabriel G. Nahas, Kenneth M. Sutin,

David J. Harvey, and Stig Agurell, Human Press, 1999. Note also that recent studies show a close correlation between marijuana use and later use of other illegal drugs, such as cocaine. A 2003 NIDA study, for example, confirmed that: "Prior marijuana use was closely associated with . . . the likelihood of young people's starting to use cocaine once given the opportunity. Among the young people who were given the chance to use cocaine, those who were already using marijuana were 15 times more likely to use cocaine than those who did not use marijuana. About 50 percent of marijuana users used cocaine within 2 years of their first opportunity to do so. However, among young people who never used marijuana, fewer than 10 percent initiated cocaine use." "Youths' Opportunities to Experiment Influence Later Use of Illegal Drugs," *NIDA Notes*, January 2003, Vol. 17, No. 5, p. 8.

8 Thomas R. Kosten and Tony P. George, "The Neurobiology of Opioid Dependence: Implications for Treatment," *Science and Practice Perspectives* (National Institute on Drug Abuse)1:1 (July 2002): 15.

9 "Social Environment Appears Linked to Biological Changes in Dopamine System, May Influence Vulnerability to Cocaine Addiction," *NIDA Notes*, January 2003, Vol. 17, No. 5, p. 10.

10 "Drug Deaths Reach a Peak as Prices Fall," *The Boston Globe* (March 22, 2000).

11 "Effectiveness of the National Drug Control Strategy and the Status of the Drug War," *Hearings before the National Security, International Affairs, and Criminal Justice Subcommittee of the Committee on Government Reform and Oversight, 104th Congress, 1st Session 14*, 18 (1995)

12 Ibid.

13 "Effectiveness of the National Drug Control Strategy and the Status of the Drug War," *Hearings before the National Security, International Affairs, and Criminal Justice Subcommittee of the Committee on Government Reform and Oversight, 104th Congress, 1st Session 14*, 18 (1995), pp. 42–43 (statement of Robert C. Bonner, former director, Drug Enforcement Agency).

CHAPTER 4: THE LINKS BETWEEN DRUGS AND TERRORISM

1 "New Pitch in Anti-Drug Ads: Anti-Terrorism," *The Washington Post* (February 4, 2002): A3.

2 See "Afghan Opium Benefits Taliban: Al Qaida Protects Heroin Smugglers, Collects Drug Tax," Michael Hedges, *Houston Chronicle*, October 3, 2001; *see also* Media Awareness Project at *www.mapinc.org/drugnews*, October 3, 2001, quoting Congressman Mark Souder (R-IN), chairman of the U.S. House Subcommittee on Drug Policy, Government Oversight Committee, "The Taliban Government and Osama bin Laden's terrorist organization al-Qaida are funded in part by the crimson opium poppies of Afghanistan, officials and experts said. 'The Afghan drug trade has given direct financial support for the Taliban . . . and at least indirectly assisted Osama bin Laden and the al-Qaida terrorist network to attack the United States,' said Mark Souder. . . ."

3 One intelligence expert put it this way: "As the bipolar world crumbled, and as the USSR was less and less able to subsidize anti-western terrorists, the classic groups exercising political violence had to look elsewhere for funding." "The New Threat of Organized Crime and Terrorism," *Jane's Terrorism & Security Monitor* (June 19, 2000).

4 "Narco-Terror: The Worldwide Connection Between Drugs and Terror," *Joint Testimony of Assistant Secretary of State for International Narcotics and Law Enforcement, Rand Beers, and Ambassador-at-Large for Counterterrorism, Francis Taylor, before the Senate Committee on the Judiciary, Subcommittee on Technology, Terrorism and Government Information*, March 13, 2002.

5 Ibid.

6 "The New Threat of Organized Crime and Terrorism," *Jane's Terrorism & Security Monitor* (June 19, 2000).

7 Ibid.

8 "Traffickers Turn from Balkan Conduit to 'Northern' Route," *Jane's Intelligence Review* (August 2001): 27.

9 "Russia Eager for Action Against Terror, Draws on Bitter Past in Afghanistan," *The Canadian Press* (September 13, 2001).

10 Ibid.
11 "Dangerous Liaisons," *Podor Magazine: Intelligence for the Business Elite*, Issue 9, June 2003, p. 9, citing a report by "Stratfor," a private "information and intelligence company."
12 "Traffickers Turn From Balkan Conduit to 'Northern' Route," *Jane's Intelligence Review* (August 2001): 27.
13 "Russia: Putin Notes Link Between Terrorism, Drug Trade," *Moscow Public Television*, FBIS Translated (September 28, 2001).
14 *The Baltimore Sun*, January 15, 2002; *see also Testimony of Steven W. Casteel, Assistant Administrator for Intelligence, Before the Senate Committee on the Judiciary*, U.S. Congress, May 20, 2003, "Narco-Terrorism: International Drug Trafficking and Terrorism—A Dangerous Mix."
15 "Three Face Drugs-for-Missiles Charge," *The Toronto Star* (January 7, 2003): A12.
16 Ibid.
17 "Canadian Accused of Smuggling Cigarettes to Fund Lebanese Terrorism," *National Post* (February 5, 2003).
18 Ibid.
19 See *International Narcotics Control Strategies Report (INCSR)* of 2002, U.S. State Department, March 1, 2003.
20 "U.S. Task Force that Tracks Down Terror Financiers to Nearly Double in Size," Associated Press (January 9, 2003).
21 Ibid.
22 Ibid.
23 *Testimony of Steven W. Casteel, Assistant Administrator for Intelligence, Before the Senate Committee on the Judiciary*, U.S. Congress, May 20, 2003, "Narco-Terrorism: International Drug Trafficking and Terrorism—A Dangerous Mix."
24 "U.S. Customs Cracks Iraqi Money Ring," Southern Newspapers (December 20, 2002).
25 Ibid.
26 "Terrorism: Questions and Answers," Council on Foreign Relations, 2003, *www.terrorismanswers.com/sponsors/iraq.html*.

CHAPTER 5: DRUGS AND TERROR AT HOME: NORTH AND SOUTH AMERICA

1 Secretary of State Colin Powell, quoted in "Powell Vows New Aid Against Narco-Terrorists," *The Washington Times* (December 5, 2002).
2 U.S. Attorney General John Ashcroft, press conference, "War on Drugs and Terrorism in Americas," Justice Department, Washington, D.C. (November 13, 2002), available online through the Department of Justice at *www.usdoj.gov/ag/speeches/2002/1302finalfarcstatement.htm.*
3 Ibid.
4 Ibid.
5 Ibid.
6 Ibid.
7 Asa Hutchinson, press conference, "War on Drugs and Terrorism in the Americas," Justice Department, Washington, D.C. (November 13, 2002).
8 ONDCP Director John Walters, press conference, "War on Drugs and Terrorism in Americas," Justice Department, Washington, D.C. (November 13, 2002).
9 Ibid.
10 See "Terrorism in Latin America," *Star-Banner* (February 15, 2002), noting "drug- and guerrilla-related violence" plagues Venezuela, Peru, Colombia, Brazil, Ecuador, and Panama, while "arms pipelines running through Brazil and Paraguay to Colombia and Peru reportedly involve Iranian-backed Hezballah terrorists"; "International Global Terrorism: Its Links with Illicit Drugs as Illustrated by the IRA and Other Groups in Colombia," *Hearings before U.S. House Committee on International Relations*, April 24, 2002.
11 *Testimony of Steven W. Casteel, Assistant Administrator for Intelligence, DEA, Before the Senate Committee on the Judiciary*, U.S. Congress, May 20, 2003, "Narco-Terrorism: International Drug Trafficking and Terrorism—A Dangerous Mix."
12 "International Global Terrorism: Its Links with Illicit Drugs as Illustrated by the IRA and Other Groups in Colombia," *Hearings before U.S. House Committee on International Relations*, April 24, 2002, pp. 1–2.
13 "Uncertain Drug Strategy," *The Wall Street Journal* (February 25, 1998): A22.
14 Ibid., p. 2; *see also* Robert Charles, "Silent Cry of Khobar Towers," *The Washington Times* (July 1, 2001), arguing before the events of 9/11/01 that "terrorism can only be stopped when exceptions are not made, when this policy is consistently applied, and when that reality is widely understood."

15 United States Department of State, Bureau of Consular Affairs, "Travel Warning: Colombia" (February 24, 2003), available online at *www.travel.state.gov/colombia_warning.html.*

16 See "Colombia: 21 Killed in Fighting Between Army, Rebels," *The Miami Herald* (January 18, 2002); "Colombian Guerrillas Kill Four," *The Washington Post* (January 22, 2002) ("Colombia's Marxist FARC rebels killed four people and blew up six electrical towers. . . ."); "Bomb Kills Three; Colombian Rebels Blamed," *The Washington Times* (January 26, 2002) ("A bomb blast ripped through a Bogotá restaurant frequented by Colombian police. . . ."); "Weekend Violence Kills 65 in Colombia," *The Washington Times* (January 28, 2002) ("The country's ascending spiral of violence continued over the weekend with 65 persons killed by right-wing paramilitary groups and leftist guerrillas. . . ."); "Colombian Senator Kidnapped," *The Boston Globe* (February 21, 2002) ("Marxist rebels forced a Colombian commercial airliner to land on a remote highway yesterday and then used a waiting vehicle to kidnap a senator. . . ."); "Colombian Soldiers Killed by Mortar," *The Washington Post* (February 12, 2002) ("In what would be their boldest attack this year, suspected leftist rebels yesterday launched a homemade mortar shell . . . killed 10 soldiers and wounded more than 30"); Peter F. Romero, "Save Colombia," *The Washington Post* (February 20, 2002) ("It's time for the United States to come to the aid of Colombia in its battle against terrorism. . . ."); "Rebels Go on Killing Rampage," *The New York Times* (February 27, 2002); "Colombia Aid Proposals Shelved: Pentagon Officials Urged Expanded U.S. Role Against Rebels," *The Washington Post* (February 28, 2002).

17 See *Hearing before U.S. House Committee on International Relations*, International Global Terrorism: Its Links with Illicit Drugs as Illustrated by the IRA and Other Groups in Colombia," April 24, 2002; U.S. House Committee on International Relations, "Summary of Investigation of IRA Links to FARC Narco-Terrorists in Colombia" (April 24, 2002).

18 See "Terrorism in Latin America," *Star-Banner* (February 15, 2002), noting that "the Spanish terrorist group ETA has been in Colombia for at least 10 years, according to the former director of the Colombian National Police, Gen. Jose Serrano."

19 See "International Global Terrorism: Its Links with Illicit Drugs as Illustrated by the IRA and Other Groups in Colombia," *Hearing before U.S. House Committee on International Relations*, April 24, 2002.

20 Ibid., p. 1.

21 U.S. House Committee on International Relations, "Summary of Investigation of IRA Links to FARC Narco-Terrorists in Colombia" (April 24, 2002), p. 2; *see also* Robert Charles, "Trilogy in the Arena of Terrorism," *The Washington Times* (November 18, 2001).

22 U.S. House Committee on International Relations, "Summary of Investigation of IRA Links to FARC Narco-Terrorists in Colombia" (April 24, 2002), p. 2.

23 Preliminary Program, DEA Symposium "Target America: Traffickers, Terrorists, and Your Kids" (December 4, 2001).

24 "Move to Link Drug, Terror Wars Draws Flak," *The Wall Street Journal* (April 1, 2002): A14.

25 CIA Director George Tenet, testimony, "Current and Projected National Security Threats to the United States," hearing before the United States Senate Select Committee on Intelligence (February 11, 2003).

26 "The Enemy Next Door," *Armed Forces Journal International* (March 2000): 40.

27 See "Colombia Under Siege," *The Washington Times* (February 9, 2002); "Colombia Destroys a U.S. Helicopter," *The Washington Post* (January 25, 2002).

28 "Colombian Report Details Drug Trafficking by Paramilitary Forces," *The New York Times,* June 26, 2003, pp. A1, A24.

29 "Public Safety Secretary Convinced Drugs 'Destroying' Mexico," *Mexico City El Universal,* Francisco Gomez and Jorge Teheran, FBIS Translated, September 26, 2001.

30 For a sampling of Ecstasy-related deaths, see "Ecstasy Blamed for Death," *The Las Vegas Review-Journal* (August 31, 2000) (21-year-old woman dies of accidental

Ecstasy overdose); "Ecstasy: Addiction Costs Teen," *The Las Vegas Review-Journal* (September 10, 2000) (Ecstasy use by 16-year-old produces brain damage; use by 21-year-old leads to death); "And She'll Be 16 . . . Forever: Mother Grieves a Year After Ecstasy Death," *The Rocky Mountain News* (January 25, 2002) (one pill leads to coma and death for 16-year-old girl on birthday); "Answers Scarce in Teen's Ecstasy Death," *The Pittsburgh Post-Gazette* (August 24, 2001) (first-time use of Ecstasy by 16-year-old results in brain damage and death); "Cops Blame Party Drug Ecstasy in Woman's Death," *Centre Daily Times* (State College, PA) (November 7, 2001) (graduate student, 23, who reportedly "didn't drink, smoke or take any drugs" dies after trying Ecstasy once); "Teen's Death Linked to Ecstasy Overdose," *The Arizona Daily Star* (April 1, 2001) (19-year-old male dead); "Ecstasy Overdose Killed N.J. Student," *The Record* (Bergen County, New Jersey) (December 12, 2001) (18-year-old male, football player, choir member, dead from Ecstasy use); "Woman Dies of Drug Overdose, Man Arrested," Associated Press (September 2, 2001) (21-year-old girl on vacation, dead from Ecstasy); "Ecstasy Caused Kent State U. Student's Death," *The Daily Kent Stater* (July 19, 2000) (Ecstasy taken at fraternity leads to "cardiac arrhythmia" death); "Two Teens Died After Ecstasy . . . ," *The Commercial Appeal* (Memphis, TN) (April 5, 2001) ("One dose can kill, doctors warn").

31 "Narco-Terrorism in California: The Middle Eastern Connection," California Department of Justice, Division of Law Enforcement, Criminal Intelligence Bureau, Group Analysis Unit (September 2002): 1.

32 Ibid.

33 Ibid.

34 Ibid., pp. 9–10.

35 Ibid., pp. 11–12.

CHAPTER 6: IDENTIFYING TRENDS IN THE DRUGS-TERRORISM RELATIONSHIP

1 See Jessica Stern, "The Protean Enemy," *Foreign Affairs*, July/August 2003, pp. 31–33; *see also The Economist*, June 7–13, 2003, pp. 11, 30; Shane Harris, "The Forgotten War," *Government Executive*, May 2003, pp. 44–54 (discussing U.S. Coast Guard role in the Drug War, hands-on leadership by Cmdr. Charley Diaz in this effort, and the drugs-terrorism link).

2 Jessica Stern, "The Protean Enemy," *Foreign Affairs*, July/August 2003, p. 32.

3 "Drugs in Central Asia: Deadly Traffic," *The Economist* (March 29, 2003): 38–39.

4 Ibid., p. 38.

5 Ibid., pp. 38–39.

6 Ibid., p. 39.

7 In the United States, 531,800 drug-related hospital emergency episodes were reported in 1995; in 1997, more than 14,000 Americans died in illicit drug-related episodes, and 3.6 million chronic drug users disproportionately spread infectious diseases such as hepatitis, tuberculosis, and HIV. *See* "Statement of Director, Office of National Drug Control Policy," hearings before the U.S. Senate Committee on Judiciary (July 23, 1997). At the same time, hospital charges for infants exposed to illicit drugs are four times greater than those for drug-free infants. *See* Joseph A. Califano, Jr., "Substance Abuse and Addiction: The Need to Know," *American Journal of Public Health* 88:1(January 1998): 9. In the aggregate, in 1995, Americans spent an estimated $57 billion purchasing illegal drugs. *See* "U.S. Drug Czar's Survey Finds Americans Spent $57 Billion One Year on Illegal Drugs—The Equivalent of a Four-Year College Education for One Million Young People," statement, Office of National Drug Control Policy (November 10, 1997).

8 In 1995, a majority of arrestees tested positive for drug use at the time that they committed the crime, and an estimated 12 million property crimes and 2 million violent crimes committed each year are drug-related. That is an estimated 280,000 reported property or violent crimes per state per year tied to illegal drug abuse. *See* "Statement of Director, Office of National Drug Control Policy," *Hearings before the U.S. Senate Committee on Judiciary* (July 23, 1997). In total, "[s]tates spent $81.3 billion dealing with substance abuse in 1998—about 13 percent of their budgets. . . ." Associated Press (January 29, 2001).

9 Cocaine is an alkaloidal narcotic derived from the South American plant *Erythroxylon*

coca and highly caustic chemicals, including hydrochloric acid and kerosene. The caustic chemical substances, which become part of cocaine as they free the alkaloid from the leaf, are mixed in thousands of jungle-floor maceration pits, creating coca paste, later to be processed into powder cocaine. Innumerable tons of excess caustic chemicals are dumped by trafficker organizations into the pristine river basins and rain forests of Colombia, Peru, and Bolivia. Similarly, volatile and dangerous chemicals used to process methamphetamine in California's mountain-forest "super labs" (and in other states) are disposed of by dumping into these chemicals into America's river basins and forests. Finally, vast marijuana tracts "ravage U.S. forests," according to recent reports. *The Los Angeles Times*, for example, has reported that "clandestine farming [of marijuana] inflicts horrific environmental damage," and endangers "visitors to public lands." Specifically, "pesticides used by the illegal growers poison wildlife and waterways, though the crop's danger is not just environmental," since "park visitors run the risk of tripping booby traps or encountering armed gangs." ("Marijuana Growers Ravage U.S. Forests," *The Los Angeles Times* [March 26, 2000]: A2). On balance, the environmental damage done by growers and processors of cocaine, marijuana, heroin, and methamphetamine are increasingly documented and regionally significant.

10 In addition to missing positive educational opportunities, side effects of substance abuse are lasting in other ways. For example, the U.S. Department of Justice estimates that 80 percent of domestic abuse is tied to substance abuse, while other experts point out that 24 to 90 percent of all child maltreatment involves substance abuse. *See* Richard P. Barth, "Substance Abuse and Child Welfare: Problems and Proposals," Child Welfare Research Center, hearings before the U.S. House Subcommittee on Human Resources, Committee of Ways and Means (October 28, 1997).

11 By way of example, 71 percent of drug users 18 and older are employed, yet these employees record higher absenteeism, more use of health benefits, more discipline requirements, and higher turnover rates. Notably, 15 to 20 percent of those on welfare admit substance abuse problems, and they remain on government welfare longer than those who are not drug abusers. *See* Statement of Director, Office of National Drug Control Policy, hearings before the U.S. Senate Committee on Judiciary (July 23, 1997); *see also* Legal Action Center (Washington, D.C.), "Making Welfare Reform Work: Tools for Confronting Alcohol and Drug Problems Among Welfare Recipients" (September 1997).

12 The significance of cost of drug addiction to America, even before calculating the burden imposed by prevention and preparation for an increase in international terrorism, is enormous. The General Accounting Office has recently estimated that "the costs of drug abuse to society—which include costs for health care, drug addiction prevention and treatment, preventing and fighting drug-related crime, and lost resources resulting from reduced worker productivity or death—are estimated at $67 billion annually." *GAO Report: Drug Abuse—Research Shows Treatment Is Effective, But Benefits May Be Overstated*, GAO/HEHS-98-72, March 1998, p. 1.

CHAPTER 7: FINDING SOLUTIONS: WHAT WON'T WORK

1 The clinical data on cocaine and heroin is widely available; less well known are the clinically established consequences of marijuana use. Consider, for example, "Clinical Consequences of Marijuana," *Journal of Clinical Pharmacology 2002* 42:7s–10s. This paper notes that, beyond marijuana addiction or "abuse/dependence, marijuana use is associated in some studies with impairment of cognitive function . . . fetal and development consequences, cardiovascular effects . . . respiratory/pulmonary complications . . . impaired immune function . . . and risk of developing head, neck and/or lung cancer. . . ." More importantly, for the current analysis, the addictive propensity of marijuana was recently confirmed by Eliot L. Gardner,

through the U.S. National Institute on Drug Abuse of the National Institutes of Health. The Gardner study found that: "Work with cannabinoids [such as marijuana] over the last 15 years . . . makes it clear that they interact with these brain processes and influence drug-seeking and drug-taking behaviors in a manner strikingly similar to that of other addictive drugs." Gardner reviewed 224 scientific papers on cannabis addiction. *See* Eliot L. Gardner, "Addictive Potential of Cannabinoids: The Underlying Neurobiology," *CPL Chemistry and Physics of Lipids* 121(2002): 267–297.

2 National statistics indicate that in 2000, driven chiefly by first-time users, "[d]rug related deaths have reached a record level in America, while users have been able to buy cocaine and heroin at some of the lowest prices in decades. . . ." ("Drug Deaths Reach A Peak as Prices Fall," *The Boston Globe* [March 22, 2000]).

3 Notably, from the mid-1980s through 1992, prices for many narcotics were driven up by coordinated supply interdiction and law enforcement efforts. At the same time, prevention messages for youth were pervasive. Attributable to these two factors were markedly lower initiation rates. "Monthly cocaine use dropped from nearly 3 million users in 1998 to 1.3 million in 1990 . . . [and] [b]etween 1991 and 1992, overall drug abuse dropped from 14.5 million users to 11.4 million." Considered from another perspective, while prices rose "[o]verall casual drug use by Americans dropped by more than half [between 1977 and 1992] . . . [and] [b]etween 1985 and 1992 alone, monthly cocaine use declined by 78 percent." ("Effectiveness of the National Drug Control Strategy and the Status of the Drug War," *Hearings before the National Security, International Affairs, and Criminal Justice Subcommittee of the Committe on Government Reform and Oversight, 104th Congress, 1st Session* 14, 18 (1995) (statement of former Acting Director of Office of National Drug Control Policy, and current Director, John P. Walters). Another expert noted that "crack-cocaine use sharply declined from nearly half a million in 1990 to just over 300,000 two years later in 1992," and "in virtually every category of illegal drug, we saw sharp declines from the mid-1980s through 1992, including "an astonishing 61 percent decline" of regular marijuana users between 1985 and 1992. "Effectiveness of the National Drug Control Strategy and the Status of the Drug War," pp. 42–43 (statement of Robert C. Bonner, former director, Drug Enforcement Agency).

4 See Avram Goldstein and Harold Kalant, "Drug Policy: Striking the Right Balance," *Science* 249:4976 ISSN (September 28, 1990): 4, 9 (legalization could affect "millions" of new users).

5 See Michael Grossman, Frank J. Chaloupka, and Charles Brown, "The Demand for Cocaine by Young Adults: A Rational Addiction Approach," *Journal of Health Economics* 17:4(1998): 427–474; *see also* Frank J. Chaloupka, Michael Grossman, and John A. Tauras, "The Demand for Cocaine and Marijuana by Youth," in *The Economic Analysis of Substance Use and Abuse*, ed. Frank J. Chaloupka, Michael Grossman, Warren K. Bickel, and Henry Saffer (University of Chicago Press, 1999), pp. 133–155.

6 "Set It Free," *The Economist* (July 28, 2001) pp. 15–16.

CHAPTER 8: FINDING SOLUTIONS: WHAT MIGHT WORK

1 Sir Francis Bacon (1561–1626). "*Nam et ipsa scientia potentas est.*" ("For also knowledge itself is power.") (*Meditationes Sacræ*, "De Hœresibus" [*Religious Meditations*, "Of Heresies," 1597]) "Human knowledge and human power meet in one; for where the cause is not known the effect cannot be produced." (*The Great Instauration*, [1623])

2 Comments from thousands of law enforcement officers would say the same thing. By example, Rick Nagel, former law enforcement officer and advisor to leading law enforcement associations nationwide, noted recently: "Support for law enforcement is essential. . . . It amounts to supporting ourselves—we cannot do without it. . . . Post-9-11, supporting our law enforcement

officers is an integral part of protection of our homeland." Interview with Rick Nagel, June 2003. That point is echoed by William J. Bennett in his 2003 volume *Why We Fight.* Bennett notes, referring to the heroism of Todd Beamer, Jeremy Glick, and Tom Burnett, whose self-sacrifice may have saved the White House or U.S. Capitol and the lives of many who live in Washington, D.C. Contrasting this act of nobility and American heroism with the cynical nihilism of the 2000 movie *American Beauty,* Bennett writes: "Nihilism is contagious, and is truly a kind of death; citizenship and mutual responsibility are also contagious, but they lead into life." William J. Bennett, *Why We Fight,* Regnery Press, 2003, p. 175.

3 By way of example, Ron Brooks, president of the National Narcotics Officers' Association, in an interview for this book in June 2003, explained: "There has never been a time when narcotics officers were more important to our nation's security, or needed more public and private support." In fact, "given the number of Americans who die each year from use of illegal drugs, trafficking in these drugs is our own, home-grown version of a chem.-bio [chemical or biological] attack on the nation." In short, the human carnage wrought and risks inherent in addressing those who do such damage are both extremely high.

4 See *The Baltimore Sun,* January 15, 2002. ("Since state-sponsored terrorism began to decline in the 1980's, the DEA has seen terrorist groups across the world—including al-Qaida—turn to drugs to help fund their activities." Still, since 9-11, law enforcement and even the National Security Agency have had to direct more focus to directly preventing terrorism).

5 A *maceration pit* is a primitive, typically outdoor, filthy, jungle-based area for processing the alkaloid component from coca leaves. These pits, an essential part of the production of cocaine, are characterized by one or more long, shallow trenches into which a variety of crude and caustic chemicals (such as hydrochloric acid, agricultural lime, and petroleum derivatives) are poured (usually underlined with plastic sheets) and into which bunches of coca leaves are then dumped. The mushy green and black brew is then stomped or mashed for a period of time, releasing alkaloids from the leaves. The resulting gooey, dark substance is then skimmed or extracted and further manipulated to create coca paste and other derivatives of the narcotic component. The bacterial and chemical impurities are processed into the paste. Rural smugglers in the pay of traffickers then transit the paste and other derivatives, often by foot, to larger processing locations, often in Colombia.

California Department of Justice, California Anti-Terrorism Information Center. "FARC-EP." *Intelligence Bulletin (Unclassified)* 13 (March 2002).

California Narcotics Officers' Association, *www.cnoa.org.*

Charles, Robert B. "Back to the Future: The Collapse of National Drug Control Policy and a Blueprint for Revitalizing the Nation's Counternarcotics Effort." *The Harvard Journal of Legislation* 33:2 (Summer 1996).

———. "California, Drugs, and Mideast Terror." *The Washington Times* (December 27, 2002).

———. "Priority Required for Protecting Utilities." *The Washington Times* (March 4, 2002).

National Narcotics Officers' Association, *www.natlnarc.org.*

"Naval Reserve Force Plays Key Role in Counter-Drug Operations." *Naval Reserve Association News* 49:2 (February 2002): 9.

Novak, Robert. "Ignoring Narco-Terrorism." *The Washington Post* (December 10, 2001).

"Oversight on United States Counter-Narcotics Assistance to Colombia." Hearing before the U.S. House of Representatives, Committee on Government Reform and Oversight, Subcommittee on National Security, International Affairs, and Criminal Justice, 105th Congress, 1st Session (February 14, 1997).

Partnership for a Drug-Free America, *www.drugfreeamerica.org.*

"Report from the Frontline: From South America to South Aurora." Hearing before the U.S. House of Representatives, Committee on Government Reform and Oversight, Subcommittee on National Security, International Affairs, and Criminal Justice, 105th Congress, 1st Session (September 22, 1997).

SAMHSA: Prevention Online, *www.health.org.*

Souder, Mark. "U.S. Congressman Mark Souder: Illegal Drugs," *www.house.gov/souder/illegal_drugs.html.*

"Terror Fight Trumps U.S. War on Drugs." *The Baltimore Sun* (January 15, 2002).

"Transnational Crime and Terrorism." *Jane's Intelligence Review* (August 2001): 55.

U.S. Department of Health and Human Services, National Institutes of Health, National Institute on Drug Abuse. "Heroin." Available online at *www.nida.nih.gov/drugpages/heroin.html.*

U.S. Department of Justice, Drug Enforcement Administration. "Afghanistan Country Brief." *Drug Situation Report* (September 2001).

———. "Heroin." Available online at *www.usdoj.gov/dea/concern/heroin.html.*

U.S. Department of Justice, Drug Enforcement Administration, Intelligence Division. "Pseudoephedrine Trafficking: The Rise of the Middle Eastern Pseudoephedrine Broker." *Unclassified Drug Intelligence Brief* (2002).

U.S. Department of Justice, National Drug Intelligence Center. *National Drug Threat Assessment* (December 2001).

U.S. Department of Justice, Office of the Attorney General. "Prepared Remarks of Attorney General John Ashcroft." (November 13, 2002). Available online at *www.usdoj.gov/ag/speeches/2002/1302finalfarcstatement.htm.*

U.S. Department of State. *Patterns of Global Terrorism 2001* (May 2002).

U.S. Department of the Treasury, Financial Crimes Enforcement Network. *Unclassified SAR Bulletin* 4 (January 2002).

U.S. General Accounting Office. "Drug Control: Assets DoD Contributes to Reducing the Illegal Drug Supply Have Declined." Report #NSAID-00-9 (December 1999).

"Ashcroft, Giuliani Open Exhibit Linking Drugs, Terror." *CNN.com* (September 3, 2002), available online at *www.CNN.com/2002/US/09/03/drugs.terror.*

Beers, Rand, Assistant Secretary of State for International Narcotics and Law Enforcement, and Francis X. Taylor, Ambassador-at-Large for Counter-terrorism. "Narco-Terror: The Worldwide Connection Between Drugs and Terror," testimony before the U.S. Senate Committee on the Judiciary, Subcommittee on Technology, Terrorism, and Government Information (March 13, 2002).

Bennett, William, John Dilulo, and John Walters. *Body Count: Moral Poverty and How to Win America's War Against Crime and Drugs.* Simon & Schuster, 1999.

Bennett, William J. *Why We Fight: Moral Clarity and the War on Terrorism.* Regnery Publishing, 2003.

Drug Enforcement Administration. "More Than 100 Arrested in Nationwide Methamphetamine Investigation." Press release (January 10, 2002).

Emerson, Steven. *American Jihad: The Terrorists Living Among Us.* The Free Press, 2002.

"The Kurdish Terrorism-and-Drugs Connection." *International Review: A Critical Analysis of World Events* (Spring 1995).

"Narco-Terrorism: International Drug Trafficking and Terrorism—a Dangerous Mix," testimony of W. Casteel, Assistant Administrator for Intelligence, Drug Enforcement Administration, before Senate Committee on the Judiciary (May 20, 2003).

"Narco-Terror: The International Connection between Drugs and Terror," speech by Asa Hutchinson, Director, Drug Enforcement Administration, at Heritage Foundation (April 2, 2002), available online at *www.usdoj.gov/dea/speeches/s040202.html.*

Stern, Jessica. "The Protean Enemy." *Foreign Affairs* (July/August 2003).

All interior images are included by permission of the author.

Robert B. Charles, attorney, educator, and former counsel to U.S. House Speaker J. Dennis Hastert, has written extensively on national security law and policy. A naval reservist who served active duty as crisis watch officer for the Chief of Naval Operations after 9/11, Charles served in the Reagan and Bush White Houses and clerked on the U.S. Court of Appeals for the Ninth Circuit. His formal education includes an A.B. in Government from Dartmouth College (1982), an M.A. in Politics, Philosophy, and Economics from Oxford University (1984), and a J.D. from Columbia Law School (1987). In 1995, he became staff director and counsel to the U.S. House National Security Subcommittee, chaired by current House Speaker J. Dennis Hastert, and served as the chief staffer to the Speaker's Task Force on Counter-Narcotics. Between 1997 and 2001, Charles taught government and law as an adjunct at Harvard University's Extension School, and received the 2000 Petra T. Shattuck Award for Excellence in Teaching. He is currently president of The Charles Group, a strategic consulting firm in Maryland. Charles is married and has two children.

Larry C. Johnson is a recognized expert in the fields of counterterrorism, aviation security, and crisis and risk management. He has worked with the CIA and served as deputy director of the U.S. State Department's Office of Counter-terrorism. In addition to his many published articles and interviews on television and radio, he has designed counterterrorism "war games" and represented the U.S. government at the OSCE Terrorism Conference in Vienna in 1996. He has played a key role in counterterrorism operations in the Middle East. Johnson currently is the chief executive officer of BERG Associates, LLC, an international consulting firm that helps multinational corporations and financial institutions manage the risks and counter the threats posed by terrorism and money laundering.

U.S. House Speaker J. Dennis Hastert rose to his position as Speaker of the House from the cornfields of Illinois. He earned degrees from Wheaton College and Northern Illinois University before teaching and coaching for sixteen years at Yorkville High School. He served in the Illinois House of Representatives for six years before being elected to the U.S. House of Representatives in 1986. In 1999, Hastert's colleagues honored him by electing him Speaker of the House, the third highest elected official in the U.S. government. Speaker Hastert is now serving his third term as speaker and ninth term as the Republican congressman for Illinois' 14th congressional district. Prior to his election as speaker, Hastert served as chief deputy whip and chairman of the House Subcommittee on National Security, International Affairs and Criminal Justice, where he conducted oversight of the Departments of State, Defense, and Justice, focusing special attention on the nation's War on Drugs.

Former Attorney General Edwin Meese was a centerpiece of the eight-year Reagan administration. He served as counselor to President Ronald Reagan from 1981 to 1985, and as attorney general of the United States for President Reagan from 1985 to 1989. He was a personal friend and trusted colleague of the president's during his early years in politics, when Reagan was governor of California. Today, Meese remains one of President Reagan's closest friends and associates. As attorney general of the United States, he was a thoughtful and formative influence in creating, gaining passage for and implementing ground-breaking laws in the areas of drug trafficking and law enforcement–related national security matters.

Former First Lady Nancy Reagan, with her husband, President Ronald Reagan, initiated one of the most significant trends in American drug abuse prevention, drawing heightened attention to this issue and coalescing parent-led groups between 1981 and 1988. As first lady, Mrs. Reagan inspired and coordinated nationwide efforts to educate youth, empower parents, and encourage lawmakers to promote meaningful drug abuse education. On this topic, she spoke at the United Nations, at the White House, in community settings, and in schools across the country. Upon leaving the White House, Mrs. Reagan founded the Nancy Reagan Foundation (subsequently part of the BEST Foundation for a Drug-Free Tomorrow). Together, these foundations have trained tens of thousands of teachers and others. Despite growing obligations in the 1990s, Mrs. Reagan took the unprecedented step, in 1995, of accepting an invitation to testify before the U.S. Congress on the issue. Her enduring message of hope and worry, concern and strength, received a warm, bipartisan reception. No first lady has done more to promote a healthy, drug-free lifestyle for America's youth.